Y0-CUY-583

THE RURAL WORLD

THE RURAL WORLD

EDUCATION AND DEVELOPMENT

Louis Malassis

CROOM HELM LONDON

THE UNESCO PRESS PARIS

© 1976 Unesco

First published 1976 by
Croom Helm Ltd
2-10 St. John's Road, London SW11
and
The Unesco Press
7 Place de Fontenoy, 75700 Paris

ISBN: 0-85664-144-8 (Croom Helm)

ISBN: 92-3-101238-X (The Unesco Press)

Printed and bound in Great Britain
by Redwood Burn Limited, Trowbridge & Esher

CONTENTS

Foreword by Edgar Faure   9

Introduction   13

1. Development and Education   27
  I. Growth, Progress Development
  II. Societies and Educational Systems

2. Integration of the Rural World into the Process of Development   51
  I. Agriculure and Development
  II. The Creation-Dissemination System in Agriculture

3. Integration of the Rural World into the Over-all Educational System   75
  I. The Basic Principles of the Educational System
  II. Specific Forms of Rural and Agricultural Educational and Integration Problems
  III. Introduction to the Programming of Rural and Agricultural Education

Appendix: Technical Note on the Quantitative Planning of Vocational Training in Agriculture   114
  I. Projection of the Working Population
  II. Determination of Training Targets
  III. Determination of Expected 'Output' and Pupil Numbers
  IV. Calculation of Costs and Capital Requirements

Notes   123

Index   126

PREFACE

In 1966 Unesco published a booklet of sixty pages or so by Professor Louis Malassis* under the title *Economic Development and the Programming of Rural Education.* Although this publication was of a rather technical character and was addressed to a fairly specialised public, it enjoyed an undeniable commercial success and, after a few years, it had sold out in French and in English and there remained only a few copies in Spanish.

In view of the abiding interest of the subject dealt with and the emphasis laid by the General Conference, at its 17th session, on the need to promote a long-term programme of education and training for rural development, it was decided, in 1973, to request the author to re-write his book in order to present a new, revised and up-dated version of it.

The author consequently set to work and started reshaping the original text in the light of the lessons he had drawn from the many missions he had effected in the developing countries during the eight previous years and taking into account recent developments in theory and practice, in particular the turning-point marked by the publication in 1972 of the report of the International Commission on the Development of Education, *Learning to Be.*

However, as the work progressed and he found himself emphasising the decisive role of rural education in meeting the needs of the Third World, Professor Malassis realised that the book on which he was now engaged would necessarily be a new work, different from the former one, with a far greater scope and intended for a distinctly wider public. In fact, he found himself considering in fundamental terms the specific problems of rural life as regards education and development.

Hence, the title of this book, in which the specifically technical aspects of occupational training in agriculture merely provide material for an Appendix.

A good number of the ideas developed in this study as well as of the principles on which it is based derive from the Report of the International Commission on the Development of Education, whose Chairman, Mr Edgar Faure, kindly agreed to write a foreword introducing Professor Malassis' book. The Secretariat would like to express here its profound gratitude to Mr Faure for this *Foreword,* which will undoubtedly help to draw the general public's attention to a study which deals with problems that are of paramount importance to our contemporaries: the relations between development and education, the integration of the rural world in the process of development, the relevance of education systems to the

---
*Professor of rural economics at the Ecole national supérieure agronomique of Montpellier; Scientific delegate to the Institut agronomique méditerranéen.

needs of evolving societies, etc.

It goes without saying that the ideas expressed by the author and the selection of facts presented in support of these ideas are the sole responsibility of Professor Malassis and do not necessarily reflect the views of Unesco.

FOREWORD
Edgar Faure, *Chairman of the International Commission on the Development of Education*

The International Commission on the Development of Education, which was established by Unesco and of which I had the honour of serving as chairman, published its report in 1972 under the title *Learning to Be,* a terse formula designed to underline the purpose of education as we should understand it today: the involvement of the individual 'from the cradle to the grave' in the unceasing extension of human knowledge.

This new concept of education required that traditional educational systems be examined from the point of view of their relevance to the needs of a world in the throes of radical transformation. We were also concerned to pave the way for a new approach in this sphere and to state common principles which could be used as guide-lines for new educational strategies.

Restricted though it was by its primary function to lay down basic directives, the Commission did not underestimate the importance of the different historical, geographic and occupational contexts within which education takes place. The finished work nevertheless called for more detailed discussion. In this respect, Professor Malassis' work admirably points the way. He has developed the themes formulated in *Learning to Be* in a particularly important area: that of the relationship between education and the rural world, which can also be seen as the relationship between education and agricultural development.

Using as his basis international statistics and FAO forecasts, the author reminds us that in 1950 some 64 per cent of the world's population gained its living from the land and that in the less developed countries this proportion will still be 55 per cent even in 1985. The problem of education will therefore, in many parts of the world, be one of rural education. A more general problem is also raised: that of a conception of culture and education which is based on analysis of the development processes and takes into consideration the needs of evolving societies.

Professor Malassis proposes that all citizens should be made aware of the role of agriculture in the economy and turns the tables on those who wish to make rural education a special category with his call for all education to be related to the rural world.

This approach is justified by the importance of agriculture in the less developed countries as well as by forecasts concerning the world food situation. Here historical models of growth in the West may prove misleading. The expansion of agriculture in Europe was indeed brought about by a mass of illiterate peasants and an élite formed of enlightened landowners and estate managers, but it would be vain to make such models a basis for action in the present. The conditions prevailing in partially developed countries today are very different from those prevailing in the West in past centuries: population growth is extremely high and the area remaining to be developed much smaller than that available to the European peasantry. Furthermore, the import capacity of the poorest states is limited and the total amount of aid extended to them by the developed nations is barely one per cent of their gross industrial product.

We are entering a hazardous, not to say dangerous, period during which partially developed countries will have to cope with a rate of population growth which it will be impossible to slow down in the short term. They will thus be obliged to rely on rapid agricultural growth although the methods used in agriculture in large areas of the world are still predominantly traditional. Zero growth is therefore out of the question as far as agricultural production is concerned. Unless they can increase their rate of growth in this sphere, partially developed countries will be unable to avoid famine, let alone to achieve industrialisation.

All citizens must therefore be made aware of the importance of agriculture in the process of socio-economic development and emphasis must be placed on training and information in country areas. A further reason why everyone should be acquainted with the problems of the rural world and country-dwellers themselves educated in a manner conducive to efficiency and social justice relates to considerations of balance and harmony between town and countryside within an overall area specially protected and adapted to human needs. The effort which will have to be put into agricultural production in the next few years should be continuously geared to the preservation of natural resources and the environment. This implies the organisation of research, experimentation and training, with a view not only to ensuring productivity but also to safeguarding the future. In more general terms, it means that mankind as a whole should bear in mind the 'new ecological dimension' and preserve the world ecosystem, to use an expression which is in common use today but which caused some raised eyebrows when I used it in *Prévoir le présent*.*

The problem of maintaining a balance between town and countryside is one which occurs in different forms all over the world. The town generates new ideas and material riches, but it can also be destructive both of nature and of social structures. In the countries of the Third World, it attracts the rural population who see it as escape from their problems. In these countries, every town has its 'poverty belt' of those who have uprooted themselves from their rural environment in the often forlorn hope of finding employment. When these people have maintained links with families still living on the land, the latter frequently help to support them. Such tragic situations could to some extent be avoided by the improvement of rural educational facilities, by the modernisation of living conditions in areas where subsistence agriculture prevails and by the organisation of reception services (for the rural population) in urban areas.

Study of rural subjects should therefore be included in education

---

*('To foresee the present')

in general, not only in order to meet the nutritional requirements of present and future societies but also to enable everyone to have a comprehensive picture of the area in which he or she lives.

The author's views on agricultural development are similar to those recently formulated by other specialists and events may bear them out. It is however difficult to distinguish temporary fluctuations from structural trends. As far as education is concerned, Professor Malassis' views are closer than would appear at first sight to certain of the basic conclusions of *Learning to Be*.

Education should be placed first and foremost in the service of democracy, which demands not only that the citizen be protected against arbitrary decisions but also that he take part in decisions which affect the future of his society. Such a state of affairs can only be achieved if all have received a basic education. If the boundaries of ignorance were to be delineated on a world map, nearly all the areas shaded in would be agricultural areas. For the rural world to be integrated within a democratic society, its education, which has already begun, must be carried further. The principle of democracy in education runs counter to the élitist conception which still holds the Western system partly in thrall and calls for the establishment of education on a broad popular basis.

The next step would be to put an end to the distinction between 'general' and 'technical' education, another legacy from the West, and to work towards a scientific and technical humanism which would enable man to understand and, if possible, control the forces which govern production and society. A general education should obviously include theoretical and practical biology and the study of man's relationship with nature and of the formation and transformation of rural communities and their relationship with the rest of society.

Education should stress the value of all mankind, developing respect for workers and particularly agricultural workers. It should demonstrate the need to increase the productivity of agricultural labour, which is the basis of all socio-economic progress, and play its part in dispelling the aristocratic view which equates work with servility.

For the educational system itself to form a whole, it must provide mobility on the vertical and horizontal planes as well as a far wider range of options. It is also necessary to do away with certain types of differentiation and segregation, particularly as regards rural and agricultural education which is all too often dissociated from the rest of the educational system.

Lastly, it is to life-long education that we must look for the key to educational policy in future years, for the educational process cannot be considered over when a person leaves school. Knowledge is continually being recreated and rediscovered as man's needs and aspirations change.

These are the principles on which the author has based his work. His examination of ways and means of applying them in a rural context leads him to a completely new vision of agricultural and rural education.

It is particularly important to give priority to life-long education in this sphere. Professor Malassis therefore sees life-long education as the arena in which the battle to decide the fate of the rural world will be fought, a view which accords with his assessment of the difficulties to be overcome in the next twenty years. For the men on whom will fall the task of increasing agricultural output sufficiently to avoid the threat of famine are more often than not illiterate adults and technicians whose present training is not fully suited to their responsibilities.

But this book is not only a list of principles applied to specific situations; the reader will also find in it the basis for a strategy designed to integrate the rural world into the general educational system during a transitional period, together with data and techniques which can be used for planning the quantitative and qualitative improvement of education and for introducing technological progress step by step within the teaching process.

International co-operation can play a major part in bringing the principles laid down in *Learning to Be* to the notice of an ever-widening public. Those responsible for the International Programme for Educational Innovation which we proposed should be evolving new approaches which could help the agricultural world to become an integral part of society and accelerate the place of rural development.

For all these reasons Professor Malassis' work is an important contribution to this high endeavour, directed to man as the agent and the beneficiary of agriculture, an endeavour which governments and international organisations should make it one of their prime concerns to pursue.

INTRODUCTION

1. The rural world

In 1950 some 64 per cent of the world's population was engaged in agriculture and in 1970 the proportion was still 52 per cent (Table 1): one man in two makes his living from the land or is a member of a farming family. The relative size of the agricultural population varies considerably from one region to another; it is related to the progress of development and is one of the many symptoms of inequality in development. In 1970, one inhabitant in twenty-five in North America was a farmer, one in five in Europe, one in three in the USSR and two out of three in Asia and Africa. In most less developed countries[1] the agricultural population considerably outnumbers the non-agricultural population and even more significant in FAO's forecast that the agricultural population will still predominate in 1985. According to the Provisional Indicative World Plan for Agricultural Development (IWP) drawn up by FAO, the agricultural population of the LDCs covered by this plan is likely to rise from 935 million in 1962 to 1,388 million in 1985 — figures which represent 67 and 55 per cent respectively of the total population (Table 2).

Although the relative size of the agricultural population is decreasing in the LDCs, *its absolute size is increasing.* One projection for Asia indicates that the agricultural population will continue to increase until about 2050; the agricultural population will then be larger than it was in 1962, even if it represents only 9 per cent of the total population.[2] The rate of increase in the agricultural population is a differential rate: it represents the difference between the rate of demographic or natural growth in the agricultural population and the rate of 'urbanisation' or movement from rural to urban areas. If the latter rate is lower than the former, the absolute size of the population will increase — although its relative size may decrease where the net rate of growth in the agricultural population is lower than the rate of growth in the urban population. Only when the rate of urbanisation exceeds the rate of demographic growth, as in the case in developed countries, does the size of the agricultural population decline both in relative and in absolute terms.

The conclusion to be drawn from this analysis, as far as our present work is concerned, is that in the second half of the twentieth century and at the beginning of the twenty-first the number of farmers requiring training will steadily increase. Towards 1985, *half the population of school-going age in the LDCs will* be members of the farming community.

The rural population, of course, is even larger than the agricultural population, for those living in the countryside include not only farmers but merchants, craftsmen, sometimes factory workers and employees of private (tourism) or public (education, health, etc.) services. Statistics on the rural population are rather unsatisfactory and above all lack comparability, for the definition of the word 'urban' varies from one country to another. The percentages available are merely rough indications valid for each country separately in the light of the definition adopted, and they do not make it possible to work out meaningful averages for large zones. Some examples can nevertheless be taken from the United Nations Demographic Yearbook (1971) which relates to 1970 or the nearest year.

Of the thirty largest African countries, twelve have a rural population of over 90 per cent, eighteen of over 80 per cent, twenty-two of over 70 per cent and twenty-seven — almost all — of over 60 per cent. In Asia, the percentage of the urban population is higher and in Latin America higher again. Out of sixteen Asian countries, seven have a rural population of less than 60 per cent. But in large countries such as India, Indonesia and Pakistan, approximately 80 per cent or more of the population is defined as rural. Although Latin America is the more highly urbanised of the less developed regions, there are roughly as many country-dwellers as town-dwellers.

Table 1. Agricultural population (in millions): Regional and world estimates in 1950 and 1970

Area	1950 Total population	1950 Agricultural population	1970 Total population	1970 Agricultural population	Agricultural population as a % of total population 1950	1970
Europe	392	128	462	88	33	19
Union of Soviet Socialist Republics	181	101	243	77	56	32
North America	166	22	227	10	13	4
Central America	52	31	93	44	60	47
South America	110	56	191	74	51	39
Asia (excluding China)	817	608	1,282	806	74	63
Africa	219	173	356	247	79	69
Oceania	12	4	19	4	29	18
Total	1,949	1,222	2,873	1,351	54	49
China	547	456	850	569	86	67
World Total	2,496	1,589	3,723	1,920	64	52

Source: FAO Production Yearbook, 1971, Table 6, p.24

Note: Agricultural population is defined as all persons depending for their livelihood on agriculture. This comprises all persons actively engaged in agriculture and their non-working dependents. In accordance with Division 1 of the International Standard Industrial Classification of all Economic Activities, agriculture is understood to include forestry, hunting and fishing.

Table 2. Agricultural and non-agricultural population and arable land per unit of population: 1962 and 1985

	Agricultural population 1962	Agricultural population 1985	Agriculture as a percentage of total population 1962	Agriculture as a percentage of total population 1985	Non-agricultural population 1962	Non-agricultural population 1985	Arable land per unit of: Agricultural population 1962	Agricultural population 1985	Total population 1962	Total population 1985
	millions				millions		hectares			
Africa South of Sahara	165	250	82	70	36	107	1.10	0.89	0.90	0.62
Asia and Far East	583	880	70	60	250	591	0.45	0.31	0.31	0.19
Latin America	99	144	44	33	127	289	1.49	1.32	0.64	0.43
Near East and North Africa	88	114	65	45	47	140	0.83	0.72	0.54	0.32
Total Zone C	935	1,388	67	55	460	1,127	0.72	0.56	0.48	0.31

Source: FAO, *Provisional Indicative World Plan for Agricultural Development: Summary and Main Conclusions*, p.14.

In the next few years, the urban population will undoubtedly increase more rapidly than the rural population; but the rural population will nevertheless continue to increase in *absolute value,* as long as the rate of movement from countryside to town (which depends basically on the rate of movement out of agriculture) remains lower than the rate of demographic growth of the rural population. Projections available for the rural population are not as satisfactory as those available for the agricultural population, but the information at our disposal makes it possible to state that *the problem of developing education in LDCs will in the next few years be basically a rural problem.*

In Africa and many countries of Asia and even of Latin America, the country school will still be that of the majority of the population.

It would therefore seem essential that *special attention be devoted to the problems of rural education* when indicative world plans or forecasts are drawn up for the development of education.

2. The rural world and economic growth

The statistics available show that the level of training of the rural and particularly the agricultural community is lower, in some cases much lower, than that of the urban community or even than national averages. In the LDCs, almost all agricultural and food products are produced by 'peasants', a large proportion of whom are illiterate and whose education, if they have received any at all, rarely goes beyond primary level.

In all developed countries economic growth occurred as a result of industrialisation fed by the transfer of resources, and in particular manpower, from agriculture to industry. The idea that development involves the decline of agriculture which becomes a relic of the past and is partly absorbed as the process of development turns the rural population into town-dwellers is one which has gained general credence all over the world. It was true of the historical process of development in the West but is not true now — nor will it be true in the second half of the twentieth century — in the LDCs, where growth rates of total population and of agricultural, non-agricultural and urban population are very different from those prevailing during the process of development in Europe. This thesis can be demonstrated quite simply by assuming two countries which have the same proportion of agricultural population (αa = 80 per cent) and non-agricultural population (αi = 20 per cent) and the same rate of increase in industrial employment (r_i = 6 per cent) and demographic growth rates of 1 and 3 per cent respectively (r_p); this can be expressed as

$r_p = \alpha_i r_i + \alpha_a r_a$ (The increase in the total population is equal to the weighted increase in the agricultural (a) and non-agricultural (i) populations.)

From this we derive:

$$r_a = \frac{r_p - \alpha_i r_i}{\alpha_a}$$

Replacing the letters by their numerical values we obtain:

$$r_a = \frac{1 - 0.2 \times 6}{0.8} = \frac{-0.2}{0.8} = -0.25 \qquad (1)$$

$$r_a = \frac{3 - 0.2 \times 6}{0.8} \quad \frac{+1.8}{0.8} = +2.25 \qquad (2)$$

In (1) the agricultural population decreases in absolute value and in (2) it increases at a rate of 2.25 per cent per annum. The situation represented in (1) is that prevailing in Europe towards the end of the nineteenth and the beginning of the twentieth centuries (the middle of the nineteenth century in England). The situation shown in (2) is that of many less developed countries at the present time: the agricultural population is increasing in absolute value. We have seen that this trend is likely to continue throughout the second half of the twentieth century and in some regions into the first half of the twenty-first. Agriculture, as measured by population, will therefore expand rather than decline.

The view that, by transforming the country-dweller into a city-dweller who is more amenable to the process of education, economic development will help to reduce the number of illiterates is therefore mistaken, as the number of country-dwellers is growing all the time. Moreover, world illiteracy figures have risen in recent years for several reasons, mainly because of the increase in the illiterate rural population. On the other hand, the process of overall development implies, more often than not, the previous or simultaneous development of agriculture: inadequate educational services for rural areas could therefore have truly catastrophic results.

Agricultural expansion in the West, which was the basis for overall economic growth, was the achievement of a mass of illiterate or poorly educated peasants and an 'élite' of enlightened landowners and estate managers (the development of the 'new agriculture' in England and its spread throughout Europe). But at that time the adjustment of agricultural growth to food demand was greatly facilitated by a low rate of demographic or natural population growth, by the reclamation of large areas in North America, Australia, New Zealand, etc., and by the net importation of foodstuffs into Europe. Present conditions in the LDCs are radically different: the rate of demographic growth is much higher and the area not yet cultivated is much smaller and much less suitable for agricultural purposes (the agricultural population is now occupying almost all the space available to it). As if all this were not enough, the LDCs are also expected to export foodstuffs in order to be able to import the capital goods necessary for their economic growth!

According to the Indicative World Plan, agricultural production would have to increase by 3.7 per cent per annum during the next few years to meet the demand for food in LDCs; this would mean an acceleration in the rate of agricultural growth, which in the 'sixties was only 2.5 per cent (and was of the order of 1–2 per cent in Europe from 1850 to 1950). The IWP expects agricultural population and total population to increase much more rapidly than cultivated area (by about 1985 agriculture will be making use of almost the whole of the potentially cultivable area in several regions of the world) and the surface available per unit of the agricultural population and per inhabitant to decrease between 1962 and 1985 from 0.72 to 0.56 hectares and from 0.5 to 0.3 hectares respectively (Table 2). In these circumstances, agricultural expansion must be based on intensification: elimination of fallow, higher cropping intensity, extension of irrigation, increased purchases by the agricultural sector (fertilisers, animal feeding stuffs, pesticides, etc.) and mechanisation and motorisation when these are seen to be necessary for a more intensive use of land. Moreover, the structure of food consumption should be changed and more stress laid on the production of protein, particularly protein of animal origin. Increased consumption of animal products means much more rapid consumption of agricultural resources (on average, seven vegetable calories are required to replace one animal calorie); traditional extensive stock-raising methods should therefore give way to more intensive methods which combine arable farming with animal husbandry.

Experiments in agricultural development carried out in the LDCs in recent years, the growth rates obtained, the world economic situation at the end of 1973, etc. lead us to the conclusion that the agricultural development which must be achieved will be an extremely difficult task, beyond the capabilities of a nucleus of enlightened landowners, administrators, estate managers and a mass of illiterate or poorly educated peasants.

In fact, it is debatable whether catastrophe is to be avoided even by improving the education and training of the agricultural population as a whole: the authors of the Meadows Report have answered in the negative.[3] Sooner or later catastrophe is inevitable, to the extent that land continues to be an essential element in the production of foodstuffs: it is the foreseeable result of exponential population growth in a finite world. Agricultural area per inhabitant will decrease (to 0.3 hectares or even less in 1985), and only an acceleration of intensification and technical progress will enable humanity to survive. In these circumstances, birth control and a decreasing rate of population growth are clearly essential, unless mankind is to exploit the world's oceans or invent new food resources.

The population explosion in the Third World marked the beginning of a new period of agriculture, which we shall call the *'transitional agricultural period'*. This period is characterised by a high rate of population growth causing a sharp increase in food demand *while the methods used in agriculture in a large part of the world are still those of the traditional period.* The transitional period therefore calls for an intensive information and training campaign designed to accelerate agricultural growth and at the same time slow down population growth.

The information and training campaign in the rural world is justified not only on grounds of the need for agricultural expansion but also by reason of the role which agriculture plays – or should play – in the process of national development, by means of the transfer of labour to industry, the accumulation and transfer of savings to help finance national development, the contribution it makes to the supply of foreign currency and the balance of payments and the part it plays in industrialisation by supplying raw materials and purchasing the finished products. These objectives can only be achieved by *increasing the productivity of agricultural labour,* which will be the starting point for expansion of the whole.

3. The rural world and development

We shall only be able to avoid starvation if we make full use of the human resources of *all* who take part in agricultural development (though even that would be no guarantee that it would be avoided). In any case, although education is an essential weapon in the war against hunger, it alone will not determine the outcome. *Development requires more than education.*

More often than not economic growth cannot take place until institutions and attitudes have undergone a change. The agricultural revolution in Europe, which was marked by a radical change in agricultural techniques, was made possible by land reforms in England (enclosure and the formation of large country properties) and by the repercussions of the French Revolution on land tenure systems. A semi-feudal agricultural system was gradually replaced by a system based on the individual worker or family. Serfdom or its consequences were abolished, joint servitudes eliminated, markets organised and gradually, as institutional credit became established, powerful cooperatives and professional organisations grew up. An agricultural system based on the family proved capable of motivating the rural worker and encouraging agricultural development, which was then used as a basis for industrialisation and the economic development of the West.

There are still areas of the world in which the *preconditions* for agricultural development are far from being fulfilled: in many countries semi-feudal forms of agriculture still exist, agriculture is practised extenisvely over large areas and peasant farmers are at the mercy of landowners, money-lenders and merchants. These archaic forms of organisation offer no incentive to the agricultural worker and at the same time restrict the development of education and the spread of progress, impeding the necessary intensification of agriculture. But the future of mankind depends on the full mobilisation of agricultural resources and public opinion will be less and less inclined to accept forms of socio-economic organisation which impede or hold back agricultural growth.

The 'green revolution', which was based on the introduction of techniques specially adapted to farming in tropical areas, and of which great things were expected, is now being to some extent held back by socio-economic problems of its own making: increased concentration of land ownership, the proletarisation of the rural world, a socio-economic infrastructure which has not changed with the times, etc.

We repeat therefore that education alone will not ensure development; the expansion of education must go hand in hand with modernisation of the socio-economic structures of agriculture. The reform of land tenure systems, the establishment of institutional credit, the organisation of distribution networks, etc., are the prerequisites for launching the process of agricultural development. In the last resort, education of the agricultural population will take on its full significance only if it is linked with efforts to bring socio-economic conditions in agriculture into line with the requirements of the modern world.

4. The rural world and education

There is a dialectical relationship between society and education: education is both the product of society and, in certain circumstances, a factor making for social change. The Western system of education is to some extent the product of the socio-economic conditions of the nineteenth century: the aim of the educational system was to produce a small number of graduates, the 'élite' which the social system needed to ensure its reproduction on an expanding scale; it divorced general education from technical education, identified general education with culture and, as there seemed to be no limit to economic growth, based general education on the analysis of historical models rather than on consideration of the restrictions to which evolving societies are subject or the inequalities of development. And it is unfortunately this Western system which, although now being remoulded, is still in many respects stamped by the past, that the LDCs use as their model. In these countries, the separation of general education from technical education is disastrous: it depreciates vocational training and manual work and foments the tradition of looking down on the rural worker, rather than emphasising the importance of agricultural work and the need to increase productivity in this sector, which is the basis for the development of society as a whole.

The historical models which have been taken over from the West project a picture of a declining agriculture, perpetuating traditional forms of life which should be outgrown if not completely eliminated, and of the new industrial, urban society which was the outcome of the process of development in the West. According to these models, the first priority is to train supervisory staff and skilled workers for the towns, rural education being postponed until a later date, as agricultural production can always be increased by uneducated rural workers as long as they are backed by competent extension services.

The effects of this approach are truly disastrous. The number of farmers will continue to increase in the LDCs and subsistence agriculture (considered by many to be an outmoded form of farming) will continue to develop; there can be no industrialisation without an all-out effort to increase the productivity of agricultural labour, a task which, for the reasons outlined above, will be incalculably more difficult than when agricultural development was achieved in the West.

The low standard of education of rural workers can be explained partly by difficulties inherent in the rural environment, but partly also by the widespread belief that economic growth can be achieved without educating the rural worker. Other reasons can also be found; the ruling classes may decide that it is not in their interest to improve the education of the rural worker; little imagination is shown in adapting the system of education to the needs of the rural world; lastly, the way of life and standard of living of farmers at present offer little encouragement to those who might wish to educate themselves.

The standard of education and degree of modernisation in agriculture appear in fact to go hand in hand. In the United States many farmers can attend courses in agriculture or business studies and in Western Europe young farmers all receive a basic education, increasing numbers going on to attend specialised courses in schools of agriculture on a full-time basis or to take part in the many short courses on general or technical subjects which are organised for their benefit; but where semi-archaic or traditional forms of agriculture prevail, there is no place for the educated farmer. In other words, a low level of agricultural development reduces the capacity for absorbing trained personnel.

If the modernisation of structures in the rural environment does not keep pace with the development of education, the latter will inevitably accelerate the flight from the land as those who have been educated will see this as the only way of putting their training to good use, of improving their income and changing their way of life.

Certain authors therefore suggest that the answer to this problem is to give the farming population an education adapted specifically to the rural way of life. Special curricula are then devised for primary schools in rural areas and the education of the farming community organised on a different basis from that of the rest of the nation, with its own establishments, its own curriculum consisting mainly of technical subjects (often overburdened with long lists and descriptions which have very little educational value), and awarding its own diplomas (rarely recognised as the equivalent of those awarded in the general system and not valid for access to higher or university education). Rural education thus becomes a ghetto, completely divorced from the general system of education and allowing no possibility of continuation or transfer. Well-informed parents will not send their children to schools which belong to this 'second-class' system of education. It will find itself catering for the worst — those who for one reason or another find other courses of action closed to them — and the best — the dedicated few who out of loyalty to their origins and a desire to change the society in which they live throw themselves into the fray with the zeal of the militant reformer.

The problems of rural development cannot be solved by educational segregation: only when agriculture itself is transformed will rural education begin to take on its real significance. Agricultural technicians will not be kept in the countryside by creating special diplomas but by giving a 'land bonus' to those who out of loyalty and conviction and the desire to take an active part in the social transformations on which development is based are willing to forego the bureaucrat's air-conditioned office: instead of 'ruralising' the education provided for the farming community, the education of the whole nation should be based on the requirements of an evolving society.

Once such societies realise that overall national development must be based on successful agricultural development, that there can be no economic growth without first transforming agriculture and improving the rural worker's productivity and that mankind is now facing a more titanic struggle to survive and develop than at any other period in its history, they will make it their duty to impress upon all their citizens the importance of agriculture and farmers and will make rural education an integral part of the educational system as a whole.

In a developing society, the aim of the educational system is to train agents of development, that is to say men who have given thought to the objectives and methods of development and who have acquired specialised knowledge in a specific field. In place of the watchword proposed by the International Commission on the Development of Education — 'towards a scientific humanism'[4] — we should prefer the formula 'towards a technological humanism', for what is needed is not so much a scholarly account of the present situation, expounded in the calm seclusion of a laboratory, as continuous action to transform it, pursued against the ever-changing background of productive forces and social relationships.

The Western concept of an 'educated man' should be rejected by developing societies; they should concentrate instead on producing people with a training at once general and technical, that is to say men who have acquired technical skill in a specific field and are able to apply it and make it relevant to the objectives peculiar to evolving societies. The barriers erected between technical and general education should be broken down, the civil service hierarchy based on other criteria than level of general education (and an academic definition of culture) and arrangements made for middle-level and field personnel to improve their qualifications and widen their experience. Education should be focused on the long-term goals and shorter-term tactics of development and should use teaching methods which place emphasis on team-work. Educational systems should learn to look to the future: although the fundamental importance of historical models for the interpretation of the present should not be neglected, models adapted to evolving societies are alone capable of providing the answers for which young people are looking, stimulating them and encouraging them to acquire the essential technical skills.

A national educational system which is based on the practical needs of development and provides the broadest possible general training, although centred on the problems of evolving societies, will produce men who are ready to play a useful part in the process of social development.

5. The great battle: life-long education

This brings us to one of the basic recommendations of the International Commission on the Development of Education: 'We propose life-long education as the master concept for educational policies in the years to come both for developed and developing countries.'[5] This is a proposal which can be justified on grounds of socio-economic and educational effectiveness and by the desire for a more just and humane society.

As we have already said, it is to illiterate farmers that we have necessarily to look to bring about the considerable increase in agricultural production which will enable mankind to avoid famine. Without adult education these men will not be able to improve their understanding of the importance and the implications of development or to acquire the technical knowledge necessary for economic growth. *Adult education is obviously more important than full-time (school) education for the success of agricultural development* during the period which we have described as the transitional period. Adult education may take several forms, from literacy work to general or technical training, and may be provided by specialised teaching establishments, by trade organisations, youth movements, political parties, etc. Its aim is not only to increase receptiveness to progress and the dissemination of new techniques: it identifies and trains the leaders of rural development, those who will be able to assume a leading role in the village communities, to the extent that they have the support of the people and the necessary qualifications for such work.

Of course young graduates leaving the schools of agriculture recently established in developing nations have a contribution to make to agricultural development. But the same should also be true of field and middle-level personnel who have generally had no opportunity of attending higher education but have often acquired considerable practical experience of development. Considerations of economic effectiveness and social justice all militate in favour of helping such personnel to accede to higher levels.

We also feel that adult education may be a more effective form of education in present circumstances. The size and complexity of the school education network have made it a cumbersome system, slow to respond to guidance or reform. The weight of tradition and the conservatism of the 'owners' of diplomas, to which certain rights and privileges are often attached, make the task of would-be reformers very difficult. The influence of the Western model, the desire to provide an education which will be the equal of that provided in the former metropolis (in order both to provide access to higher education in the metropolis and to acquire the rights and privileges conferred by certain diplomas), the difficulty of evolving a new system of education which is suited to the historical and geographical circumstances of each country and to the requirement of its development, etc., often make full-time education in developing countries a conspicuous failure as far as the process of development is concerned.

Adult education, on the other hand, is a new departure which allows full scope for creative imagination and innovation: new institutions and methods must be devised, real needs identified and understood and men with direct experience of the problems of developing countries involved in discussion at all levels. The result might be a new vision of culture and technology, very different from that projected by the structures of the school system.

The aim of life-long education is to create not only a more efficient but also a more just society. It should make it possible to offset the effects of social origin on career prospects by giving all men at some moment in their lives the opportunity to acquire the general education and technical know-how required for certain posts. This is important in every country, but particularly so in the LDCs.

Life-long education should also mean a more humane society. It offers the individual *several chances of success* in the course of his life: failure at school no longer means a *life sentence* to the 'ghetto of one's own failure'.[6] It also makes it possible to change direction once or several times, as dictated by the expansion of the economy and in particular by the need for occupational mobility which this process implies, or in accordance with the rising level of individual and group aspirations and expectations. Young nations could make life-long education the basis of their educational system: it would enable them to evolve a form of training adapted to their own needs and less conditioned by their past and Western models.

Life-long education, an essential ingredient of national development, seems to us to be one of the bases of agricultural development too, both for the reasons outlined above and because the rural world has been particularly affected by under-education, academic segregation, historical models and mistaken conceptions which have for a long time equated general education (in its traditional forms) with capacity for socio-economic development.

Life-long education could thus become the basic principle on which the whole edifice of the national education system is built. But one point should first be made clear. If education is to be considered an instrument enabling the individual to continue to make progress through his life, it must be a process which has *already started.* Although if there is to be life-long education the individual must be able to attend whatever course he wishes, at any place and at any time, this in itself is not enough. Life-long education implies that both young people and adults should have acquired a primary education or basic training which will enable the process of education to be continued. We therefore see three separate sub-systems within the overall educational system: school and university education, basic training for adults and the further training of adults of adults or life-long education proper.

6. General outline and plan

This work will develop the themes outlined in this introduction. As uneven development has become one of the major problems of socio-political philosophy in our time, we shall consider the relationship between development (growth, progress) and education; we shall then discuss the integration of the rural world into the process of development and of rural education into the overall educational system, touching at certain points on the ruralisation of the overall educational system. We feel that the objectives, structures and methods of the educational system should be based on prior analysis of the objectives and methods of development, so that it can be made to serve the needs of evolving societies. This does not of course mean that we should not draw on the store of past experience or neglect the lessons to be derived from historical processes; what it does mean is that we must also pay attention to the requirements of the future and in particular to the efforts which will have to be made to produce enough food to support mankind and to conserve and use our natural resources to the best advantage.

Our original intention was, at the request of Unesco, to bring up to date our previous publication *Economic Development and the Programming of Rural Education* (Unesco, 1966). The many missions to LDCs which we have had the opportunity to carry out over the last ten years, and even more important, the changing approach to such problems crystallised in the publication of the International Commission on the Development of Education's seminal report, have in fact led us to revise the original work so completely that this is in fact a new publication.

The Commission's report was the document which we used as the basis for our considerations. Many of the ideas and principles contained in this work are indeed to be found in *Learning to Be* or proceed from it. However, our interest in the rural world sometimes led us along different paths to those followed in that report. It is our earnest hope that the present work will stimulate constructive reactions and suggestions and we should like to thank in advance any reader who will be so good as to write to us at the address given below.[7]

We should also like to thank all those who in one way or another have helped in the preparation of this work and in particular Mr Carrel of Laval University (Canada) and Mr J. P. Frémeaux of the Institut Agronomique Méditerranéen, Montpellier (France), who were kind enough to read through the manuscript and make comments and suggestions.

CHAPTER 1. DEVELOPMENT AND EDUCATION

1. GROWTH, PROGRESS, DEVELOPMENT

A. Growth

1. Unequal growth: the distribution of world economic growth

First-hand experience and reference to the relevant statistics both make it clear that economic growth is unevenly spread. Whatever criteria are used — production figures or national product, income, consumption, savings, standard of living indicators connected with the basic economic objectives of human activity (to provide food, training and information, medical care), etc. — *considerable differences* emerge between one country and another and, within the same country, between different races and ethnic groups, different sectors of activity, socio-occupational groups, regions, etc.

With the aid of growth indicators, 'scales of growth' have been established and the countries of the world divided into two basic groups which are described as the rich and the poor, the developed and the less developed or the advanced and the backward countries, depending on one's conceptual or ideological point of view. Although neither the system of classification nor its terminology is universally accepted, it has been the starting-point for many studies and publications in recent years.

In fact, the term 'uneven growth' can have two meanings: unequal access to material goods at present and unequal increase in material goods available per inhabitant in recent years. Inequalities in growth rates widen the gaps between developed and less developed countries. Uneven growth has become one of the major problems of contemporary socio-political philosophy. This is partly due to awareness of the *growing disparities* but also and above all to the fact that underdevelopment is seen to be *morally unacceptable* since scientific analysis has shown that growth margins exist and experience has proved that *per capita* growth in LDCs is possible given the right circumstances. If poverty is not due to the avarice of nature or to man's fall from grace after disobeying the Almighty but rather to our institutions and our ignorance, *the battle for development and education can be joined on an objective basis.*

However the 'Club of Rome' has recently drawn attention to the factors limiting growth and to the dangers humanity is now facing (Meadows Report).[1] In its representation of the way in which mankind is moving, the Meadows Report focuses on the consequences of exponential growth in a finite world. Five basic factors are taken into consideration: population, capital, food, non-renewable natural resources and pollution. The report's conclusion is clear: 'The basic behaviour mode of the world ecosystem is exponential growth of population and capital, followed by collapse'.[2]

Although much criticised, this representation has the great merit of encouraging public opinion to be more orientated towards the future and less towards the past.

It helps to create an awareness of international interdependence within the world ecosystem and places the phenomenon of economic growth in its true geographical perspective. Pointing out the tragic consequences of *irrational, uneven exploitation* of natural resources, it calls upon the richer nations, 'the pillagers and polluters',[3] to exercise more restraint. It is obvious that a general deceleration in growth does not afford the means of reducing world disparities between different standards of living and would merely perpetuate present imbalances in growth. *The basic problem facing humanity is therefore the distribution of the world growth margin between the different sub-groupings of the world ecosystem.* To narrow the gap between developed and less developed countries requires a reversal of recent trends, with *per capita* growth higher in the LDCs than in the developed countries.

2. *Overall growth and* per capita *growth: the distribution of world population growth*

Per capita growth is a differential rate of growth: it is the difference between the rate of growth in the economy as a whole and the rate of population growth.

Let us take: P = population
Y = production
y = production available per unit of population

and r_P, r_Y and r_y as the rates of growth. (Variation shown as a percentage in population, total production and *per capita* production respectively.) Then we can say:

$$Y = P.y$$

and deduce $\quad r_Y = r_P + r_y \quad$ (formula 1)

— a formula which is satisfactory for relatively small variations, or

$$r_y = r_Y - r_P \quad \text{(formula 2)}$$

— a formula which clearly demonstrates the diffential nature *per capita* growth. This approach can be illustrated by the following model which shows recent trends:

Category of country	r_Y	r_P	r_y
(1) Less developed countries	5	2.5	2.5%
(2) Developed countries	4.5	1	3.5%

This model shows that *per capita* economic growth has been more rapid in developed countries (3.5 per cent) than in LDCs (2.5 per cent) although overall growth was higher in the latter (5 per cent) than in the former (4.5 per cent). Thus the gap between developed and less developed countries has widened.

This could lead to hasty conclusions, ready-made solutions to solve the troubled conscience, for example the reaction 'all we need to do to reduce disparities in economic growth is cut back population growth in LDCs'. Of course another child means another consumer to enjoy the fruits of growth, but it also means another producer to bring this growth about. We should therefore try to assess how the marginal productivity of labour is affected by introducing additional producers into the production system.

If N is the number of workers and W average production per labour unit, we can write:

$$\frac{Y}{N} = W \quad \text{or} \quad Y = N.W$$

$$\text{so} \quad r_Y = r_N + r_W$$

$$\text{and} \quad r_W = r_Y - r_N \quad \text{(formula 2)}$$

For purposes of simplification, we can assume growth in the productivity of labour (r_W) to be equal to growth in production available per unit of population (r_y). This means simply that growth in the total population (r_p) must equal growth in the working population (r_N), or in other words that the proportion of working population to total population must remain constant.

The above formula can be used as a basis for consideration of three different situations:

1. $r_p = r_Y$: The population is increased at the same rate as production the marginal productivity of labour is zero ($r_W = r_y = 0$) and production available per unit of population remains constant. The economy is expanding in absolute terms but stagnating in terms of its relationship to population.
2. $r_p < r_Y$: Production available per unit of population is increasing in proportion to the marginal productivity of labour.
3. $r_p > r_Y$: Although production is increasing in absolute terms (r_Y being positive), the marginal productivity of labour is decreasing, as is the production available per unit of population.

When the question of *per capita* economic growth is analysed, the basic problem is not necessarily that of population growth but that of the productivity of labour. The answer to the question regarding the origins of poverty, one of the bones of contention between Goodwin and Malthus, is to be found in an analysis of the factors governing the marginal productivity of labour.

If economic growth per unit of population is small or non-existent, this may be the result of excessive population growth in relation to economic growth. But low economic growth is not necessarily the result of poverty: it may be due to an inability to promote progress, to expand education or to off-set the social factors impeding development. An effort should therefore be made to devise and apply structures, means and methods which would make it possible to optimise the productivity of labour, although this may necessitate social reforms or even radical transformation of the socio-economic system.

However, even if optimisation of labour productivity is a *fait accompli*, it does not follow that it is desirable to even necessary to reduce population growth. Such reduction may be desirable with a view to distributing economic growth more evenly between quantity (r_p) and quality (r_y) of life, although r_y obviously does not include all aspects of quality of life.

In the long run population growth is bound to decrease, given exponential increase of the human population in a world with limited resources. 'In 1650 the population numbered about 0.5 billion, and it was growing at a rate of approximately 0.3 per cent per year. That corresponds to a doubling time of nearly 250 years. In 1970 the population totalled 3.6 billion and the rate of growth was 2.1 per cent per year. The doubling time at this growth rate is 33 years.'[4] According to the Meadows Report, the factors which will decide our future — capital, food, non-renewable natural resources, pollution — are limits which will inevitably impose birth control policies. *The population problem is therefore how to distribute population growth between the different sub-systems of the world ecosystem.* This problem is no whit less important than that of the distribution of overall economic growth.

3. The role of education in reducing inequalities in growth

Consideration of inequalities in growth is based on the international comparison of countries classified according to carefully chosen indicators.

The explanation for inequalities may be sought in *internal structures and behaviour patterns:* available resources, population, socio-economic system, methods of production, mental outlook and behaviour patterns, cultural and educational systems, etc. In general, there is a positive correlation between levels of training and information and growth levels. But the basic question is whether education is a cause or an effect of development. In fact it may be both: the product of society and, in certain circumstances, an instrument of social change.

Although it is true that the less developed countries have much lower levels of education than developed countries, it would be wrong to conclude that all that is needed to achieve *development* is *education*.

In fact, economic growth depends on a large number of variables of which education, although necessary, is only one.

An explanation of inequalities between different countries may also be sought in *international relations*. Here international solidarity is at fault, particularly at a time when, as we pointed out above, the problem of growth is becoming more and more one of the distribution of the growth of mankind as a whole within the world ecosystem.

The present situation may be explained by reference to historical processes, the relationship between dominating and dominated nations and the resulting obstruction of development, and the transfer of the profits on increased productivity in the LDCs to developed countries by means of unfair international trade patterns. The educational process has also played its part. The colonial powers usually organised the educational systems of the LDCs in such a way as to help them to meet their need for middle-level personnel and skilled labour; research and extension work in agriculture was designed to improve the yield of agricultural products and raw materials for export rather than to meet the real needs of the country's development, etc.

Any policy for aid and co-operation which, among other things, encourages transfer of technological know-how, makes it possible to improve standards of training and information, organises research with a view to regional and world development and seeks to end the migration of talent will obviously help to reduce present inequalities in growth.[5] Care must be taken above all not simply to transfer educational systems, techniques and thought patterns from one country to another but to help to adapt them and introduce new approaches to education and technology which are more in accordance with a particular historical and geographical context. If inequalities in growth are to be reduced, one of the first priorities must be to reduce inequalities in the productivity of labour. There is no doubt that the reduction of inequalities in education is a means towards an end.

However, uneven development is not caused only by inequalities in productivity: it can also result from the machinery for *distributing the fruits of improved productivity*. Here we refer to social structures and economic mechanisms: ownership of the means of production, the mechanisms whereby income is accumulated and distributed (prices, wages, profits), the existence of mechanisms for redistribution (social security), the level of unemployment and unemployment benefit, etc. Blatant inequality in the distribution of profits will lead to the formation of conservative social attitudes in those who have benefited from the system and to the resignation or revolt of the masses.

The division of the fruits of world economic growth between the nations is a burning question. There are two schools of thought: the 'relative advantages' theory, according to which international division of labour should make it possible to increase world economic growth to a maximum, and the theory of 'unequal exchange' which perpetuates phenomenon of unequal growth. In recent years deterioration in the terms of trade between developed and less developed countries has meant that the former have benefited from increased productivity in the latter. This situation has been denounced by many authors, both Marxist and non-Marxist, and is the central preoccupation of UNCTAD (United Nations Conference on Trade and Development). However, the recent rise in raw material prices gives rise to a new situation.

Economic growth depends on factors other than education, such as social change, international relationships and world development. However, education plays an important role in promoting technical progress, which is a basic factor of growth. We shall therefore consider education as a factor of technical progress before taking a more general view of the relationships between society, social trends and education.

B. Progress

1. Factors of economic growth: the role of technical progress

Economic growth (r_Y) is directly dependent on a number of factors — in particular labour and capital — which we call the factoral components of growth. It is indirectly dependent on a large number of other factors connected with the system of socio-economic organisation and more precisely on its capacity for change, which will affect the components of growth.

Let: N = number of workers r_N = growth in N
       K = available capital r_K = growth in K
       Y = national product r_Y = growth in Y
       $\frac{N}{Y}$ = labour coefficient in the process of production =
       $\frac{K}{Y}$ = capital coefficient

Initially, the growth in national product can be shown as equal to growth in the factors of production (weighted according to their relative importance in the production process):

$$r_Y = \alpha r_N + \beta r_K \qquad (1)$$

However, the results of applying this formula to various national economies as they have developed in recent years do not bear it out and show that allowance must be made for a 'third factor', also called the 'residual' factor (R), bearing in mind the process used in this calculation:

$$r_R = r_Y - (\alpha r_N + \beta r_K)$$

This third factor corresponds to the increase in overall productivity of the factors (labour and capital), which is a way of measuring *technical progress*.

Growth in national production is not only a result of growth in employment and in the other means of production; it is also the result of technical progress – of the process whereby more and more refined methods are used, new and better-educated generations of workers begin to take part in production, life-long education is implemented, changes are introduced in the socio-economic organisation of production, etc.

Progress is therefore a specific variable of growth, and recent studies have *even shown it to be the main variable of growth in Western economies* (Table 3).

Table 3. Average annual growth rates, 1950-60

	r_Y	r_N	r_K	r_R
United States	3.3	1.1	0.8	1.4
North-west Europe	4.8	0.8	0.9	3.1

According to this table technical progress acounts for 1.4/3.3, i.e. 42 per cent, of growth in the United States and 3.1/4.8, i.e. 60 per cent, of that in North-West Europe.

These refined methods of analysis, which are admittedly open to question as regards certain aspects of the procedure employed and certain of the findings, presuppose the availability of reliable statistical data and can only be usefully applied to relatively homogeneous economies: such figures are not available for the LDCs. However, despite the lack of overall figures there is much evidence of the decisive role played by technical progress in increasing production.

2. *The mechanisms of technical progress*

Technical progress is achieved by a system leading from *creation* to *dissemination*. The basis of economic growth, overall and *per capita*, is the growth of productive forces which in turn is based on the discovery of the laws governing nature and societies, the invention of new techniques, methods and forms of organisation, the practical application of discoveries and inventions and their dissemination throughout the socio-economic system.

The inventors on whose work the economic growth of the West was based were practitioners rather than 'scientists' in our sense of the word. As the amount of knowledge has increased and production processes have become ever more complex, the basis of creation and propagation has become education. A schematic representation of the process leading from creation to dissemination is given in the diagram on the following page.

```
                                    ┌ Discovery
                   ╱── Creation    ─┤ Invention
                  ╱                 └ Development
        Education
                  ╲                 ┌ Information
                   ╲── Propagation ─┤ Innovation
                                    └ Dissemination
```

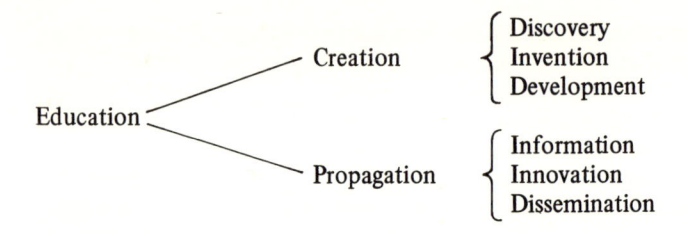

Let us illustrate this diagram by an example chosen from agriculture. The *discovery* of the laws of heredity led to the *invention* of new varieties (of cereals, for example). These had to be grown on an *experimental* basis, in order to determine their specific characteristics (in particular their yield), the conditions in which they could be used and the desirability of propagating them. Discovery, invention and experimentation are the successive stages in the process of creation, which can also be described by the expression 'Research and Development' or R and D. The varieties chosen must then be *propagated*. Farmers must first be *informed* of the existence of these varieties and of their performance (show farms). Some will decide to grow them themselves and will thus be *innovators,* agreeing to use a new means of production. If they are successful, they will be followed by the cautious majority and use of the new varieties will gradually be *disseminated* to cover the whole of the area suitable for their cultivation. Information, innovation, dissemination are the three successive stages in the process of propagation.

The system leading from creation to dissemination is a coordinated group of linked operations which are all necessary for increasing the productivity of factors, from both a functional and a structural point of view — and consequently for speeding up economic growth — and which can only be understood and made more effective if considered as a whole.

The *progressive society* is one which seeks to organise and develop education and the creation and propagation of new forms, to speed up the rate of discovery and application of new techniques, and to shorten the time which elapses between the different stages leading from creation to dissemination. Our age is characterised by a 'great leap forward' in our potential for creation and propagation.

> Science and technology have never before demonstrated so strikingly the extent of their power and potential. During this 'second twentieth century' knowledge is making a prodigious leap forward. Research and innovation are being institutionalised, while change is accelerating boundlessly, as is the capital of human knowledge and the number of people working in science. (More than 90 per cent of scientists and inventors in all of human history are living in our times.) Equally remarkable is the constantly diminishing gap between a scientific discovery and its large-scale application. Man took 112 years to develop practical applications of the discovery of the

principles of photography. Only two years separated the discovery from the production of solar batteries.[6]

Education plays a decisive role in the emergence of a progressive society: it helps to train research workers by handing on to them the sum of knowledge accumulated so far and instructing them in the use of scientific methods while, by encouraging a creative approach, it makes the population at large more receptive to change, raises the general standard of information, reduces the time lag between creation and innovation, etc. Education is the foundation on which a progressive society can be built. However, the effectiveness of an educational system depends on its objectives, its methods and its structures.

3. *The process of creative destruction*

According to J. Schumpeter, growth is a process of creative destruction. This process is spurred on by technical progress. The railway destroys the stage-coach and obliges coachmakers to find other jobs but, at the same time, it makes it possible to carry more goods and more passengers faster over longer distances. As an invention, it both creates and destroys goods and services. At the same time, however, it affects men's activity, forcing upon them an occupational mobility which may take the form of movement from one region to another and involving problems of employment, retraining and the severance of ties with the social environment. In a progressive society, efforts are made to reduce the human cost of technical progress or to offset it by establishing machinery to facilitate occupational and social mobility.

When the rate of technical progress accelerates, as it has done in our time, adaptability becomes a major human requirement. A system of education which focuses on the acquisition of technico-vocational skills *during the period of schooling* loses all meaning, for a man may need to change his job several times in the course of his working life or to engage in activities which has not been dreamt of when he was at school. Life-long education then becomes a socio-occupational necessity.

The economic expansion of the West was based on industrialisation, whose characteristics are greater use of mechanical energy, a higher ratio of technical capital per labour unit and the invention of methods and forms of production which make it possible to ensure a continuous increase in the productivity of labour. This process has now reached a level where mass consumption is possible despite inequalities in the distribution of wealth.

But many other important changes took place in Western society in course of the process of industrialisation: the expansion of capitalism, the relative increase in size of the wage-earning population, the flight from the land, the expansion of services, urbanisation, the disintegration of the family as a production unit (the different members taking different jobs) and as a social unit, changing institutions, higher individual expectations, growth and transformation of the educational system, etc.

The relationships between technology and society are dialectical; technology is a product of society (the pace and form of education, research and information), but the growth of productive forces destroys ways of life and institutions, makes necessary permanent alterations or radical changes in socio-economic systems and creates new generations whose aspirations and behaviour are different from those of their forebears.

C. Development

1. Traditional societies

Technical progress may be considered the basis of the process of economic growth and social change. Depending on the rate of increase in overall productivity and particularly in the productivity of labour, it is possible to distinguish two types of society: those in which productivity increases slowly or very slowly are called 'traditional' societies and those with rapid growth are called 'progressive' in view of the importance of technical progress as a component of growth.

Traditional societies are basically agricultural societies: agriculture is their main activity and the appropriation of goods and services produced by this sector is the main source of wealth and power. In such societies the basic variable of the process of growth and development is the population variable, as it determines the volume both of consumption and of production (labour-based economy).

In a traditional economy the volume of production depends on the number of workers and the surface area under cultivation (yield per unit of surface area remaining fairly constant from one year to the next). When the population increases, cultivated surface area will expand as long as land is available (growth by extension). When all available land in a given zone is being used, human settlement can expand no further and surface area available per worker begins to decrease (growth by labour-based intensification). This traditional type of growth within a limited area can be divided into two main periods, each of which has several phases.[7] The first, the period during which food production outstrips requirements, we shall call the pre-Malthusian period. The second, during which food production lags behind the increase in population, tends towards the catastrophic phase described by Malthus.

Traditional economies are not necessarily poverty-stricken: in the olden days it was possible to have full granaries and plentiful flocks as well as a large family of children and grandchildren. These economies are nevertheless at the mercy of natural phenomena and are subject to severe though short-lived famines.

However, if there is a considerable reduction in the amount of surface area available per worker as a result of population growth, without an accompanying change in production techniques, a drop in the marginal productivity of labour may result, with an ensuing tendency towards famines becoming structural and, paradoxical though this may seem in societies which lack material goods, towards unemployment or underemployment. In such circumstances, the most powerful social groups seize land to safeguard their own position and to subjugate the mass of the population. This is the case in feudal and semi-feudal systems where the great lords own the land and exercise considerable power over the individual, whether on a *de jure* or a *de facto* basis. These 'landowners' distribute both land and employment, life and death, ruling over a destitute and hopeless people who have no independent means of production and, in apparent subjection, depend for everything upon their masters.

At some stage in the process of traditional growth, there is usually a fierce struggle for the ownership of land. At different stages and in different contexts, different types of agricultural society have evolved which can be classified into two main types on the basis of their attitude to land: those based on an egalitarian distribution of land, centring in varying degrees on the community (the so-called community or tribal societies, etc.), and those based on appropriation of land, of which the feudal society is the most typical and the most widespread.

2. Progressive societies

A traditional society may become a progressive society as a result of successive reforms or of violent, radical and revolutionary change. In Western Europe, the 'take-off' process in England was facilitated by changes in the economy and new land structures while the French Revolution destroyed the feudal system and made the whole of Europe receptive to social change. Industry-based liberal capitalism, which formed the framework within which take-off and subsequent development in the West occurred, is based on a process of industrialisation deriving from the Industrial Revolution in England and the gradual spread of liberal ideas.

The process of Western development was also based on changes in agriculture which made it possible to increase the productivity of agricultural labour. These changes were both technical (with agricultural extension work playing a decisive part) and social: the abolition of serfdom, changes in the laws affecting ownership of land, abolition of joint servitudes, organisation of markets and credit facilities, etc.

Agriculture was a crucial factor in the take-off of the Western economies, particularly those of England and France, but it was itself transformed by the process of Western development. The transformation of agriculture can only be properly understood if it is seen in the light of the process of overall development. It can be explained in terms of two major variables which are external to agriculture: the growth of monetary demand for food products and the demand for the transfer of manpower from agriculture to non-agricultural sectors of the economy. An understanding of the role of agriculture in the process of overall development is as essential for the 'general' student who wishes to understand the process of social changes as a whole as for the agricultural specialist who wishes to affect the course of agricultural development.

Western expansion in the LDCs brought about radical transformation of traditional societies and often destroyed them completely. The conquest of Latin America in the sixteenth century, the colonisation and settlement by Europe in the nineteenth century, etc., caused great upheavals. European expansion changed the attitude to land throughout the world. It replaced community or semi-community land tenure systems in Latin America by feudal systems, established peasant (and more rarely, semi-feudal) agriculture in North America, introduced capitalist forms of ownership in many countries (plantation farming) and gave rise everywhere to the idea of individual landed property.

Traditional societies were also changed by the introduction of non-agricultural activities, on Western initiative. Plantations and factories call for manpower, or lead to forced labour systems, involving changes of activity and population migration, sometimes on a very large scale. The monetarisation of the economy, concentration on exports, urbanisation and the beginnings of industrialisation are all factors making for the transformation of traditional societies, introduced on Western initiative.

Settlement by the West gave rise in the LDCs to dualist societies. This dualism was not only economic but also cultural. The West introduced its own languages, its educational systems, its beliefs, its ideologies, etc. Having attained independence, and now faced with the task of enabling their economies to 'take off' en route for development, the LDCs do not have merely to build up an economic system but also, and more fundamentally, a society of their own, choosing their own way to development and their own blueprint for society. The creation of an educational system favouring economic growth and social development will stem from this blueprint for society.

2. SOCIETIES AND EDUCATIONAL SYSTEMS

A. Education and society

1. *Education, a product of society*

There is a dialetical relationship between society and education: education is both the product of society and, in certain circumstances, a factor of social change. Seen from the angle of socio-economic development, education is an historical category, linked with the different stages of this development. The objectives, content, methods and scope of a system of education can be determined by examination of its relationship with society.

It is clear that the different forms of education result from different socio-economic systems or methods of production. The diverse types of society, whether patriarchal, slave-based, feudal, capitalist or socialist, have systems of education which differ from each other in varying degrees. In traditional societies, the elders hand down to the younger generation all they need to know to ensure their livelihood and the continuity of their family, clan and tribe. Although the traditional society has no school, this does not mean that it has no education. In progressive societies, however, the rate of change and the growing complexity of production processes are such that education becomes institutionalised and the school becomes the symbol of a developing society. However, the main object of schooling is to acquire knowledge; it does not cover the whole of the educational process: family, physical surroundings and social environment all continue to play a fundamental role.

In every society, the different forms of education socialise and reproduce culture. The generation in power hands down a legacy of ideas and techniques to the rising generation. The educational system is strongly influenced by the past and the social context and tends to reproduce existing situations: 'Education, being a sub-system of society, necessarily reflects the main features of that society.'[8] A society based on authority and injustice cannot be expected to produce a fair, liberal system of education. Schooling reinforces prevailing ideologies, whether dictated by the ruling class or inspired by recent independence or a successful revolution. Education thus 'helps to consolidate existing structures and to form individuals for living in society as it is. Therefore, and we do not mean this pejoratively, education is by nature conservative.'[9]

2. Historical processes and education

The phenomenal socio-economic transformation of the West can be explained basically in terms of growth and development. Strange though it may seem, *analysis of the processes of development,* of their objectives, their mechanisms and their agents, has never been an explicit objective of the Western educational system.

Development took place without the educational system devoting attention to it as such. The educational system supplied a need for education which was linked with the process of growth and aimed to create an 'élite' of 'educated men', technicians capable of applying their knowledge to specific tasks and a labour force trained to carry out repetitive work on a production chain.

All Western systems of education offered two alternatives: 'general' education and 'vocational and technical' education. The *parting of the ways* occurred very early, at the age of eleven or twelve, and was inevitably decided to a large extent by social origin. General education provided the only access to university and the leading specialised institutions of higher education; this was how one became an 'educated man' and basically this was also reserved for members of 'good families'. Vocational and technical education was for the 'practically minded' and the ordinary people.

A 'general' education or an education in the 'humanities' presumed to identify itself with 'culture' and this led to a rather contemptuous attitude towards technical, vocational or manual training. The 'educated man' was primarily the product of a classical education whose sources were the past history of mankind, Greek or Latin literature, Western and Eastern history, rather than an education which, while allocating due importance to the past experience of humanity and historical *processes,* also devotes attention to analysis of contemporary situations and, better still, to the construction and analysis of models of *evolving societies,* and which *incorporates technology* as a pre-condition for growth and development.

Education in the West still bears the imprint of nineteenth-century concepts: it has shown little capacity for internal renewal and adaptation to social changes and the changing aspirations of the younger generations. On the other hand, the dimensions of the educational system have kept pace with the process of development (linear growth). Western society is gradually acquiring a 'mass education' system and this widening of the stratum from which pupils and students are recruited is no doubt not unconnected with the younger generations' criticism of the system.

For the first time in history, pupils have begun to reject the products of institutionalised education. 'A system designed for a minority — when knowledge was slow to change and man could, without undue presumption, hope to "learn" in a few years everything to satisfy his intellectual and scientific needs — quickly becomes out of date when employed for mass education in times of whirlwind change and when the volume of knowledge increases at an ever faster pace.'[10]

The educational systems in developed countries are therefore undergoing a crisis; the same is true in the LDCs, but in a very different historical context and for different reasons. ' . . . seen across the prospect of time . . . nothing seems to have had more significant consequences for the world than the mark and orientation which the colonising Europeans left on modern education in Latin America, Africa and vast reaches of Asia.'[11]

After their experience of educational systems used to promote the aims of the colonialist powers, the newly independent colonies made the Western concept of the 'educated man' their ideal and imported systems of education which divorce general from technical education, downgrade vocational and manual work and are often based on class distinctions and used to reproduce existing social structures. They also concentrated on full-time (school) education and paid relatively little attention to adult education or classes designed to enable people to improve their qualifications, which would have been a way of training leaders to adopt a practical approach to development problems rather than an academic approach that has never had much place for analysis of development process anyway! Analysis of the objectives and mechanisms of development tends to be reserved for the specialists — yet development is not the business of specialists, it is the business of the people themselves, educated in the problems of development and trained to deal with them.

3. Education, a factor of social change

Education is manifestly the product of a society; it is strongly influenced by historical processes. Although a product of society, education can also be an instrument of social change, but this only under certain conditions, the most essential of which are the relative independence of the educational system from the political authorities and a guarantee of freedom of expression for teachers and pupils. Even when these basic conditions are fulfilled, it is still an open question whether the educational system is capable of reforming itself without reforms in the society which has produced it — in other words, whether it is capable of exerting pressure upon the social environment. There are two extreme schools of thought, one of which, the 'social determinism' school, holds that the educational system is utterly incapable of reforming itself or of putting pressure upon society, while the 'voluntarist' approach considers education to be the main instrument of social change.[12]

For agricultural development, it is obviously necessary to train and inform the farming community, but this is not enough. Other factors are involved, such as land reform, changes in the organisation of distribution networks, the establishment of institutional credit, etc., all of which proceed from changes in the structure of society. The voluntarist school of thought would thus appear to be based more on make-believe than on facts. More than education and much more than instruction is required for development. But the critical analysis which may be encouraged by a *liberal* educational system can contribute towards a new awareness and provide the impetus for reform. The educational system is also the basis for technical progress; as such it is an instrument of creative destruction, and its effect on society is cumulative.

While education appears to have followed the process of development in the first Western countries to become industrialised, this does not seem to have been the case in the United States, Japan or the USSR. And although neither its methods nor its content are perfect, the immense amount of effort that has gone into education in the Third World in recent years will no doubt bear fruit.

B. Educational systems

1. Definitions and trends

In the context of the historical development of the West, given the pace of technological change, the growing complexity of production systems and the rising level of expectations and aspirations, education became a nation-wide institution and the school the symbol of a developing society.

In both developed and less developed countries, but for different reasons, the concept of education is now beginning to extend far beyond the original framework of the school, taking a comprehensive view of the needs of the whole population and the various ways in which they can be met: the school continues and probably will continue in the next few years to play a fundamental role in the process of training but its role as educator is tending to become less prominent[13] as is its role in establishing a social hierarchy — a development warmly welcomed by Illich,[14] and many others, including ourselves.

We use the term *'educational system'* to denote a combination of institutions and methods whose object is to raise the educational level of the whole population of a given country and which may intervene at any stage of an individual's life, with a view to encouraging and adapting the process of national development and assisting in the development of the individual. This is an ambitious view which cannot be said to correspond to reality: all that can be detected at the moment are tentative moves in the direction of life-long education.

Life-long education should not only give each individual the opportunity of acquiring whatever training he wishes at any time; it also implies the previous acquisition of basic skills (literacy), i.e. it implies that the educational process has already begun. This leads us to identify three separate sub-systems within the educational system as a whole, namely school and university training, basic training for adults and further training for adults. The school and university sub-system includes pre-school, primary, secondary and higher education. The sub-system providing basic training for adults is for those who did not have the opportunity to acquire a basic training at school (or were not able or did not wish to take advantage of it at that stage). It offers essentially training in literacy (school, functional or mass). The sub-system providing further training for adults, or life-long education in the true sense of the word, implies a continuing educational process based on elementary skills which have already been acquired either at school or through basic training for adults. As we have seen, the arguments in favour of life-long education are partly socio-economic and partly considerations of social justice and humanity.

The structure of the educational system as a whole can be described in terms of the relative sizes of the three sub-systems (perhaps on the basis of the years or year-equivalents spent in training). These proportions will depend on the historical and geographical contexts and on the strategies and policies adopted. The educational system cannot be considered to form a unified whole unless the three sub-systems are genuinely co-ordinated with a view to achieving the society's educational aims and are, in consequence, interdependent.

An educational system is a historical category associated with the stages of development and at the same time a geographic category associated with the socio-political ideology of the different nations. However, at the present time, some general principles are emerging on which agreement is almost unanimous, although their implementation may be delayed by difficulties of one sort or another. In a word, the tendency now is towards the establishment of educational systems which can be described as overall or global (involving the whole population of a social unit), diversified (to deal with specific situations or needs), open (to provide genuine equality of opportunity), encouraging adaptability (aptitude to learn, additional training and retraining) and able to play an effective part in social development (inventiveness and the critical analysis of development mechanisms).

2. *The diagnosis of educational systems*

On the basis of what has been said above, analysis of an educational system would seem to involve consideration of the system *as a whole,* of its overall objectives (democratisation, mobility, development), of the relative size of the sub-system of which it is composed (pre-school and school education, basic training for adults, life-long education proper) and the relationships between these sub-systems, of the resources allocated to education and their distribution, of the methods used and the results obtained. Most of these questions are analysed in detail in the report of the International Commission on the Development of Education; we shall therefore merely draw attention to certain points which appear to be particularly relevant in this context:

1. Present educational systems are not particularly well geared to the objectives of socio-economic development either in content (development is hardly ever a teaching subject, general education is divorced from technical education, etc.), in structure (predominance of the school sub-system, specialised nature of establishments, lack of opportunity for career guidance and reorientation) or in methods (traditional teaching methods etc.).

2. Attendance rates and levels of education are still low. The situation in 1968 has been described as follows:

> Universal school enrolment at the primary level has been virtually achieved in some developing countries and in the industrialised nations. Some of the latter have a secondary school attendance in excess of 70 per cent, the most advanced reaching 90 per cent. Yet more than half the total population of developing regions have never been to school, less than 30 per cent of their young people go to secondary school and less than 5 per cent go on to higher education.[15]

Although the number of illiterates throughout the world has decreased in relative terms (from 44 to 34 per cent between 1950 and 1970), it has increased in absolute terms (from 700 to 783 millions);[16]

3. Education appears to be relatively ineffective as far as economic development is concerned (because the educational system is not geared to the objectives of development). However, this is a matter which it is difficult to assess. The internal efficiency or output of the system, as measured by the number of pupils who begin a course divided by the number of those who complete it, is also manifestly very low. The quotient is 2 in Africa, 1.9 in Latin America, 1.3 in Asia and 1.2 in Europe.[17] 'In half the countries of the world, half the children enrolled in schools fail to complete the primary cycle.'[18] School wastage, which includes drop-outs and repetitions of grades, adds unnecessarily to the average cost of each fully educated pupil.

4. Levels of education and school attendance rates differ considerably according to ethnic group, race, sex, region or area and socio-occupational category.

'With about one third the population and only one quarter of the young people in the world, industrialised countries spent *ten times more* money on education than the developing countries.'[19] From 1960 to 1968, expenditure on education increased more rapidly in developed countries than in LDCs, which means that the gap has widened. Disparity between the sexes is particularly marked in the LDCs. In Europe, North America and Latin America, enrolments for girls and boys in primary and secondary schools were more or less equal, but in Africa, Asia and the Arab States, there are 50 per cent more boys than girls in primary schools and 100 per cent more in secondary schools.[20]

Disparities between the different socio-occupational groups can be observed by comparing the proportion of skilled workers, administrative grades and intermediate-level personnel in the working population with the proportion of children from these different socio-occupational groups who actually gain access to education. There are also often considerable disparities between regions, and between urban and rural areas. Regional statistics for education show considerable differences, sometimes 50 per cent more or less than the national average.[21] Educational facilities are often concentrated in urban areas, to the detriment of rural areas. In Latin America for example, 59 per cent of village schools offer only a two-year course; 6 per cent of primary schools in rural areas offer five full years of elementary education as against 66 per cent in urban areas.[22]

It is a fairly well-known statistical phenomenon that children whose parents belong to different socio-occupational groups do not have the same chance of access to education. This phenomenon is particularly noticeable in higher education, as shown by the following table:

Table 4. Enrolment in higher education by parents' occupation

	Liberal professions and management		*Workers*	
Country	Students (as percentage of total enrolment)	Group (as percentage of total active population)	Students (as percentage of total enrolment)	Group (as percentage of total active population)
Japan	52.8	8.7	8.7	44.2
United Kingdom	62.9	21.5	27.2	71.5
United States of America	52.4	22.9	26.6	57.4

Source: Edgar Faure *et al.*, *Learning to Be,* (Unesco-Harrap, 1972), p.73

5. Although results have been rather unsatisfactory as regards levels of education and enrolment rates, effectiveness and efficiency, democratisation, etc., the cost of education has risen continuously and is now an almost unbearable burden for some LDCs. The *public* cost of education varies between 3 per cent of gross national product (Latin America) and 6 per cent (North America).[23] It is rising more rapidly than GNP and budget expenditure as a whole, of which it therefore represents an increasingly large proportion (3 per cent of world GNP in 1960 and more than 4 per cent in 1968; 13.5 per cent of budget expenditure in 1960 and approximately 15.5 per cent in 1967).[24] Although in half the countries of the world only half the children who attend school complete their primary education, the latter accounts for 20 to 40 per cent of public spending.

6. Education is facing a crisis which calls for a more creative and original approach to objectives, structures and methods and consequently to the distribution of the sums allocated for education. However, what has happened in recent years is that the system has progressed in a linear fashion, simply be reproducing itself on a larger scale, rather than by introducing radical changes.

3. The 'intellectual investment' system

We use the term 'intellectual investment system' to refer to the expenditure which enables a society to provide for research (R), training (T) and extension work and information in general (E).[25]

$$I_i = R + T + E$$

Although the term 'intellectual investment system' is rather unsatisfactory on several counts, we have not been able to find a better formulation of the concept. Education in the widest sense is in fact both an 'investment' and a form of 'consumption', which increases an individual's capacity for production while at the same time developing his personality and satisfying his need to know and understand. This formula does however take into account the three fundamental components of the process leading from creation to dissemination, emphasising their interdependence and drawing attention to the problems in regard to co-ordination and the distribution of financial resources.

If the productivity of labour rises in a given society and savings therefore increase by, say, one per cent, should this increase be invested in material goods or in human intelligence? Or should it be divided — and if so in what proportion — between these two types of investment? Similarly, in what proportion should financial resources be divided between research, training and information? Or between the three educational sub-systems? Although these questions arise frequently we are still not able to give scientific answers to them. To do this, we should have to evaluate and compare the results likely to be obtained from these alternative forms of investment. In a model which takes economic growth as its main objective, we should need to evaluate the contribution likely to be made by these different types of investment to value added. In a model whose objective is 'development', there would be many parameters and the optimisation criteria would be difficult to define, many of them being non-economic. In fact material and intellectual investments should be regarded as complementary rather than rival types of investment. For example, the construction of a dam which will enable land that was farmed dry to be irrigated, radically changing agricultural production systems throughout the area, will require some accompanying investment in research, training and information.

In general, nations tend to spend much more on material than on intellectual resources. Material investment probably represents 15 to 20 per cent of the GNP of advanced nations while 'intellectual' investment represents from 5 to 10 per cent. The structural distribution of intellectual investment between R, T and E is difficult to assess. Attempts to define the content of each of these types of intellectual investment and to evaluate total expenditure (both public and private) on each category come up against numerous difficulties.

For a long time now production units in advanced societies have kept their capital equipment up to date by means of a *sinking fund,* the amount of which is determined not by the probable lifetime of the asset in question but by the period within which it is likely to become obsolescent. The increasing pace of technical progress hastens the process of destruction and increases depreciation payments and net investments: the cost of material progress is continually rising.

It is not only material equipment that needs to be discarded and renewed; the same is also true of the knowledge accumulated by the individual at school. When the rate of progress accelerates, one can no longer hope to equip one's children with a capital of knowledge which will last them all their lives. If the same system were applied to intellectual capital as is now applied to material capital, there should be a system of annual contributions levied on gross turnover which would enable the workers of the firms in question to keep their vocational knowledge and skills up to date. This would involve production units in the financing of 'refresher' courses for their workers. What is really needed however, is a completely new form of 'social security'. Until now, State insurance and security systems have catered for stoppage of work for physical reasons, accident, age, illness, etc. But in a society where economic growth is accelerating and the process of creative destruction disrupts as it improves, other forms of insurance and security are called for which will enable the individual to keep his professional skills up to date or to acquire new ones, and thus to maintain his job or his ability to work. In a society which is experiencing rapid economic growth, with the changes which this involves, the basic problem is not to keep one's job but to have a job. The objective should not be to base the future on knowledge and skills acquired at school, i.e. on a diploma (for all qualifications tend to lose their value in a period of economic growth), but to keep professional skills up to date by constant retraining. A developed society can soften the impact of material and intellectual change by assuming responsibility for an increasing proportion of the costs involved.

Technical evolution makes life-long education a duty rather than a right. But the concept of life-long education involves far more than the depreciation and renewal of assets or even social security: it also involves education as consumption, a means of satisfying personal needs and developing the human personality. The concept of an 'intellectual investment system' does not only involve expenditure on schooling and schools. It covers everything that is done, whether by individuals, production units, local bodies or the central authorities, to provide training for all those who request it, wherever they may live and whatever their age.

In the LDCs the task of adapting the intellectual investment system to development raises many problems. Looking back on the sacrifices they have made for education in recent years and the results they have obtained, these countries are bound to reflect on the comparative profitability of intellectual and material investments *and also the socio-economic effectiveness of the different forms of education.* Consideration of the mounting costs of education, which they are finding it increasingly hard to bear, together with the low internal efficiency of the educational system, the growing number of educated unemployed and the mass of illiterate workers, inevitably leads these countries to reappraisal of their educational policy.

4. Educational systems and rural development

If one examines educational systems in their relationship to the rural world and agricultural development, the following facts emerge:

1. General education pays scant attention to the war being waged against hunger, to the role of agriculture in the development process, to the need to improve the productivity of farm work as the basis for overall growth and ways of achieving this improvement or to the relationship to be established between industry and agriculture in the process of overall growth and social change. LDCs have been no more successful than developed countries in creating a mode of education which is geared to socio-economic development and combines the essential ingredients of such development – technical, economic and social – within a single, integrated course. This type of training would be invaluable for evolving societies; agriculture, as an important growth sector, and rural societies, which provide the sociological basis for the creation of new societies, would naturally be included as subjects for study. The present situation may be explained by the Western concept of training for an élite, by lack of interest in agriculture which is felt to be an occupation with no future, perpetuating traditional forms of life which should be discarded, and by general lack of understanding of the needs of evolving societies.

Concentrating as they do on traditional, general types of training, the educational systems of the LDCs produce too many 'administrators' for rural areas who openly proclaim that they 'don't know the first thing' about agriculture', partly to excuse themselves and perhaps above all to set themselves apart. They pass as 'educated men', having been raised on foreign literature, historical processes, legal rules, etc., but they are sometimes incapable of conducting a logical discussion on the processes of agricultural development and hence on the processes of overall development and the social transformation of their country.

2. Agricultural training, like all technical training, is more often than not a separate entity quite distinct from general training. As we have said, the educational system of all Western countries used to offer two alternatives: general education, turning the children of 'good' families into 'educated men', and technical and vocational training, for the 'practically minded' and, almost exclusively, the 'ordinary people'. Despite the efforts of reformers in developed countries to reduce the influence of social origins, to improve the general training of 'technicians' and open the doors of the university to them, the process of integration is still not complete.

The younger nations bear the marks of the educational heritage of the West: more often than not they have maintained an education system which separates general from technical education, downgrades vocational and manual skills and makes the educational system a class system used to reproduce existing social structures. Training for agriculture is thus provided in special establishments (schools of agriculture, agricultural secondary or grammar schools, etc.), which issue their own diplomas, which are seldom recognised as being equivalent to those of general education, and do not permit access to university or other forms of higher education. Agricultural education is therefore an educational ghetto, having no links with general education and offering no opportunity for choice or transfer. In such circumstances, this type of education cannot be called 'a sub-system' of the educational system as a whole: it is a closed system on its own.

3. The rural population is in general less well and in some cases much less well educated than the average citizen. Although this is true throughout the world, the disparities are particularly acute in the LDCs. This situation may be explained by the difficulties inherent in rural life, but these could probably be overcome if there were not other, more intractable problems. In fact, the reasons for this state of affairs are unfavourable socio-economic structures, the defence mechanisms instituted by favoured social groups who may find it to their advantage not to improve rural education, the general belief that the peasant farmer does not need to be educated to provide us with as much food as we want and the style and standard of life offered by rural communities at the present time.

The standard of education in rural areas is low because access to education is poor and those who have been educated tend to leave agriculture. This cause-and-effect link between education and the flight from the land is grist for the mill of those in favour of 'ruralising' agricultural education: we have already stated our views on this subject and will revert to the point at greater length at a later stage.

4. Despite the efforts made in recent years in the LDCs, much criticism has been levelled at the system of agricultural education itself. FAO refers to the phenomenon of the 'inverted pyramid' or the 'potentially acute shortage in the supply of intermediate personnel'[26] and more generally of 'field technicians'. 'On the qualitative side, many of the present products of agricultural education are criticised because of inadequate academic standards, the irrelevance of much of the subject-matter taught, the totally inadequate training in practical farming and in understanding the farmer and his problems, and an inability to communicate with farmers.'[27]

5. The success of vocational training for farmers is basically determined by the organisation and effectiveness of the process leading from creation to dissemination in agriculture, a process combining training, research and extension work.

Agricultural extension services played a decisive role in the development of agriculture in the West and similar services have been established in all the LDCs. They should be made more effective, however, by increasing the number of extension workers deployed per unit of area, improving their training, adapting the methods used and involving farmers in their operation as far as humanly possible. The creation-dissemination system has a crucial role to play in the agricultural development of the LDCs and we shall devote several pages to this system in Chapter 2.

6. Agricultural extension services may be regarded as an ingredient of life-long education for farmers, to the extent that they help to bring new methods to their notice and encourage them to use such methods more widely. They also contribute to socio-economic development by establishing appropriate institutions (co-operatives) and providing leaders for the basic community units (community development). Although the LDCs have often made strenuous efforts to promote basic education (functional literacy) — and even life-long education — for adults, it is by no means certain that a too scholastic approach has not been adopted to rural training and the opportunities offered by adult education underestimated. Efforts to help people improve their qualifications are in most cases patently inadequate.

7. By analogy with the overall system of intellectual investment a system of investment in agriculture and rural development could be formulated as follows:[25]

$$I_a = R_a + T_a + E_a$$

This formula expresses the division of expenditure between research, training and extension work in agriculture.

It is illuminating to know in what proportion this expenditure is distributed: in developed countries, research and training tend to predominate whereas in the LDCs more may be spent on extension work. The distribution of financial resources is an important factor in the strategy for rural development. However, this strategy must be regarded as one strand in the nation's scientific and educational policy, particularly where agriculture is closely integrated with the life of the nation as a whole. To put it another way, the process leading from creation to dissemination in agriculture depends both on 'general' factors (g) (basic research, national educational system, socio-economic information) and on the specific needs of agriculture (a) (agricultural research, agricultural training, agricultural extension activities):

$$I_a = R_{g+a} + T_{g+a} + E_{g+a}$$

In the following pages, we shall analyse the present situation (diagnosis of educational systems) and resolutely take up a position for the integration of rural education in a comprehensive approach to the whole educational system and to the creation-dissemination system in general. But as the educational system should in our view proceed from the system of development, we shall first consider the integration of the rural world in the general development process.

CHAPTER 2. INTEGRATION OF THE RURAL WORLD INTO THE PROCESS OF DEVELOPMENT

Development strategy and educational strategy

The object of Chapter 2 is not to examine in detail the integration of agriculture into the development process, as this subject has already been dealt with in another Unesco publication.[1] Integrated agricultural development will be taken more as a basis for reflection on the definition of an educational system which is geared to the objectives of development. 'The concept of integrated agricultural development means viewing agriculture not as a separate sector but rather as a branch of the economy completely integrated into the development process and contributing to the fulfilment of the objectives which society as a whole has set for itself.[2]

Agriculture and the economy as a whole, rural communities and society as a whole, are interdependent: agriculture often plays a decisive role in economic 'take-off' but overall economic growth in turn brings about important changes in the agricultural economy — by increasing monetary demand for foodstuffs, creating non-agricultural employment requiring a transfer of manpower from the countryside to the towns and creating demand for producer and consumer goods in the agricultural sector, whose purchasing power tends to increase. Analysis of the process of development therefore places considerable emphasis on the relationships between agriculture and industry. In pre-industrial societies where almost the whole population earns its living from the land, the type of farming engaged in is necessarily subsistence farming; during the process of overall development, agriculture becomes more market-orientated; in fully industrialised economies agriculture itself tends to become industrialised, that is to say, to adopt the methods and structures of the industrial economy.

It is clear from these few examples that an education which concentrates on agriculture will fail to convey an understanding of the changes taking place in this sector and that, in the same way, a 'general education' which does not include analysis of the part played by agriculture and the farming community in the establishment of a new economic and social order will give a distorted view of socio-economic realities. Training to take part in general development should therefore be given not only to those responsible for promoting and supervising agricultural development but to all attending school and, on an even wider basis, to the whole population, for all are affected by the process of development. To be more precise, development stems from the national consciousness and the national will, and thus calls for training and information which will help these to cement. But, as we have already said, the sort of instruction manual which could be used to introduce an education of this kind is at present noticeable for its absence. Although development has been the

51

subject of many works published in recent years, they are in the main written by specialists for specialists or deal only with certain apsects of the question and cannot be regarded as 'textbooks' giving a coherent, comprehensive and graduated basic training.

In the course of our many missions to many different countries, we have often been struck by the fact that those responsible for promoting and supervising agricultural development had received only a very rough-and-ready training and in some cases no training at all on the mechanism of development. In the light of this situation, we were asked by Unesco to write a work on the 'integration of agriculture in development' which could be used as a reference manual for the drafting of national textbooks adapted to more or less specific historical and geographical contexts. Readers wishing a more detailed examination of the relationships between agriculture and industry within the development process should refer to that work.[3] In the present chapter we shall restrict ourselves to discussion of certain basic aspects, as they impinge on the educational system.

I. AGRICULTURE AND DEVELOPMENT

A. The emergence of a progressive agriculture

1. Underdeveloped societies

Underdeveloped societies are still farming societies and the agricultural economy continues to play an essential role in them, both by its contribution to the formation of gross domestic product and by its contribution to exports (Table 5). One of the basic characteristics of the LDCs is their dualist structure, inherited from the past when traditional societies were virtually taken over by Western societies and their economies orientated towards the supply of raw materials (minerals) and agricultural and food products for export to the West.

The average productivity of agricultural labour is low in the traditional sector; and although relatively high in the modern sector, productivity in the agricultural sector as a whole is low and progressing very slowly. There are many explanations for this state of affairs: semi-archaic or traditional forms of socio-economic organisation in agriculture (tribal, semi-feudal, peasant), the small cultivable area per labour unit in certain zones, low levels of mechanisation and investment in equipment and the small amounts of fertiliser, pesticide, etc. purchased. Very often the socio-economic system does not provide any incentive for agricultural expansion as the benefits of increased farm productivity are milked off in part by landowners, merchants and money-lenders. Where levels of training and information are fairly low, it is natural to suppose that production could be increased if farmers were better educated. But although, as we have said, improved educational services are a necessary condition for agricultural growth, they are not sufficient in themselves. Let us assume, for example, that extension services have taught the farmers to make use of fertilisers and that sufficient supplies of fertiliser are available. If, because of high land rents, exorbitant interest on loans and fluctuating prices, the use of fertilisers were to increase the farmer's feeling of insecurity instead of reducing it, threaten his precarious financial equilibrium and risk involving him in debt, the farmer would justifiably reject the advice of the extension services and, given the socio-economic context in which he was operating, this would be perfectly rational behaviour.

Table 5. Agriculture as a source of income and employment in 1962

Regions	Agricultural population (% of total population)	Agricultural GDP as % of total GDP	Agricultural exports as % of total exports
Africa South of Sahara	82	40.3	59
Asia and Far East	70	37.4	60
Latin America	43	20.4	49
Near East and North-West Africa	65	24.7	18
LDCs	67	29.4	43

Source: FAO, *Provisional Indicative World Plan for Agricultural Development: Summary and main conclusions,* (Rome, 1970), p.2.

In these circumstances, the introduction of new techniques is directly dependent on prior changes in the socio-economic pattern of production. Such changes may include land reform, the establishment of institutional credit, the organisation of marketing networks involving guaranteed sales and stable prices, etc. The prevailing type of agriculture in the LDCs is a customary, semi-feudal or traditional, peasant agriculture in which farmers are exploited in a number of different ways, not one of which is likely to encourage the development of a progressive agriculture; indeed, this may be impossible without prior social reform or revolution.

2. The Green Revolution

Considerable progress has been accomplished in the West since the Second World War and this has made it possible to accelerate agricultural growth. Recently agricultural progress has mainly taken the form of improvement of plant and animal species, the discovery of high-yielding varieties, fertiliser techology, plant protection, water technology, etc.[4] A new phenomenon which holds particular promise for the LDCs is the discovery of techniques suitable for use in tropical regions, based in particular on high-yielding plant varieties. This new technology is the basis of what has come to be called the 'Green Revolution'.

The research work undertaken in Mexico by the International Maize and Wheat Improvement Centre and in the Philippines by the International Rice Research Institute played a key role in launching this revolution. In Mexico, average wheat yields went up from 0.94 tons per hectare in 1949 to 2.64 tons in 1968. In the Philippines, the cultivation of new varieties is expected to double yields. These varieties are now being grown in various parts of the world, and particularly in India, Pakistan, Turkey and Tunisia. Between 1965 and 1970, the area sown with these varieties increased from approximately 20,000 hectares to 15-20 million hectares.[5] Although these varieties were the basis for the Green Revolution, increased yields also reflect higher inputs of other production factors — fertiliser, pesticides, water, etc. The success of this new technology is not to be disputed and it has given rise to great hopes for the future but it is also clear that it raises serious socio-economic problems.

1. Use of the new varieties has tended to concentrate in the most favourable areas, where land structures are satisfactory, farmers are able to acquire the new means of production (new seeds, fertilisers, pesticides, etc.), marketing structures are well organised and so on. In the early stages, therefore, the new technology will tend to accentuate regional disparities and as competition becomes more intense the position of less favoured regions may deteriorate.

2. Within a given area those who have benefited most from the new technology are usually the 'large' farmers, which means that social disparities have been accentuated rather than reduced. Larger farmers are often more receptive to technical innovation, more educated and up to date; they benefit most from the extension services, which single them out for special attention for that reason, and they have capital or access to credit, etc. The new technology therefore tends to emphasise the heterogeneity and in particular the dualist nature of the agricultural economy: large, productive farms thrive and the small farmers mark time.

3. One of the advantages of the Green Revolution is that it creates employment as agricultural production becomes more intensive. Thus in the Punjab (India) agricultural demand for manpower increased more rapidly than the agricultural population.[6] But in some cases, increased income has encouraged large farmers to introduce mechanisation, which reduces the number of agricultural jobs. Moreover, when the technological revolution takes place within a context of underemployment, wages remain at the bare minimum. In Mexico, where the Green Revolution began in the 1940s, from 1940 to 1960 the average growth rate of agricultural production was 5 per cent a year. From 1950 to 1960, however, the average number of days worked by a landless labourer fell from 194 to 100, and his real income decreased from $68 to $56. Eighty per cent of

the increased agricultural production came from only 3 per cent of the farms.[7]

In order to put the new profits of the Green Revolution to good use, landowners tend to evict smallholders or sharecroppers who, until then, farmed their land for them, in order either to farm it themselves or to charge a more profitable rent. Successful farmers are also able to purchase more land from which they evict the smallholders and so on. The end result *is that the proletarisation of the rural world is increasing rather than diminishing.* The study carried out by the FAO Special Committee on Agrarian Land Reform 'confirms the already widespread impression that an improvement in productivity alone does not make life any easier for the mass of rural workers but on the contrary often makes it more difficult.[8]

4. The Green Revolution has only affected certain areas of the world, the boundaries being determined not only by agronomic but also and more importantly by socio-economic factors. There can be no Green Revolution where training and information services are inadequate or unsuitable, where land structures are restricting, where access to credit is costly, where the distribution organisations are unable to provide a guaranteed market for increased production, while diverting to their own pockets part of the profits accruing from the increased productivity, – in short where the technological revolution does not benefit those who are responsible for bringing it about and does not therefore offer them any incentive.

It is clear that a purely technological 'Green Revolution' does not tackle the problems of the distribution of income or social justice any more than that of the accumulation and circulation of money within the social fabric and its consequences from the point of view of overall development. It does not create the conditions for mobilisation of the population in general, which imply that those responsible for increased productivity should be able, at least in part, to reap the benefits. Agricultural training and advice on the use of the techniques of the Green Revolution are not sufficient if the socio-economic structures as a whole are not geared to the process of development. What we need is a comprehensive approach to development, covering all its aspects, technological, economic and sociological.

3. The role of agriculture in overall development

The specialists agree that agriculture can contribute to overall economic growth and development in four ways:

1. By increasing the volume of agricultural and food production in proportion with the growth in internal and external demand;
2. By the transfer of resources, labour and capital from agriculture to other sectors of the economy, thus contributing to overall growth if (and *only* if) the productivity of the factors transferred is higher outside

the agricultural sector than within it;

3. By contributing to the supply of foreign exchange and to the balance of payments, to the extent that exports of agricultural and food products exceed imports. The foreign currency obtained from net exports can be used to import the capital goods needed to modernise the economy;

4. By contributing to the process of industrialisation, either through supplying raw materials for the agricultural and food industries or through purchasing industrial goods, thus stimulating the process of industrialisation and overall growth.[9]

The effective contribution of agriculture to economic growth depends on the role which is allocated to it within the overall process of growth.[10] Agriculture can be a 'leading sector' in development: in such cases, it must produce the surplus which will feed the whole process of development. Agriculture can also be an 'adjustment sector': in such cases, the economy is launched more by non-agricultural sectors – extractive industries (petroleum), manufacturing industries (textiles), services (tourism), etc. Agriculture must then adjust its transfer of resources (manpower and capital) and of products (growth in the monetary demand for food) to the rate of growth in non-agricultural sectors, in order to avoid disequilibria which may hold back or even block the process of overall growth.

Whatever the nature of the role entrusted to agriculture in the development process, it will only be able to fulfil it if the productivity of agricultural labour can be increased. This is desirable in order to:

1. Improve the nutritional standard of the rural population;

2. Increase the number of mouths which can be fed by one farmer, as a result of the transfer of agricultural manpower towards industry and the relative decline in the agricultural population. When the agricultural population represents 80 per cent of the total population, the number of mouths fed by one farmer averages 1.25; when the agricultural population has dropped to 20 per cent, the average is five (transfer effect);

3. Increase the *per capita* income of the urban population as the process of development progresses and increase monetary *per capita* demand for food (income effect);

4. Increase exports of agricultural products to the extent that agriculture must produce the foreign currency which will make it possible to import the producer goods necessary to launch the process of industrialisation (development effect).

In view of the cumulative effect of these factors and the rapid increase in the total population (exponential demographic growth curve), agricultural development implies a process of increasing intensification which will make it more difficult to increase the marginal productivity of agricultural labour.

B. The outlook for agricultural development

1. The Indicative World Plan for Agricultural Development

In 1970 FAO published a 'pioneering' study in the field of international perspective planning: the Indicative World Plan (IWP).[11] The object of this plan is to throw light on the future, to measure agriculture's ability to play its role in world development, to contribute towards an awareness of the basic problems raised by agricultural development and to guide agricultural policies.

The plan was based on an estimate of probable demand for food, bearing in mind the projected increase in population and *per capita* demand. This increase has been estimated at 3.7 per cent per annum for the LDCs from 1962 to 1985 although it was only 2.6 per cent from 1960 to 1968 (2.1 per cent in Africa). The foreseeable increase in food demand *therefore implies an acceleration of agricultural expansion in the next few years.* To this internal expansion should be added an increase in agricultural exports, to the extent that they have a contribution to make to the overall process of development in the LDCs. The main trends identified by the plan as far as the LDCs are concerned can be summarised as follows:

1. Although decreasing in relative value, the agricultural population will continue to increase in absolute value. For the LDCs as a whole, the agricultural population will decrease in relative value from 67 to 55 per cent between 1962 and 1985 but will increase by almost 50 per cent in absolute value, rising from 935 to 1,388 million (Table 2). Examination of trends in Asia has shown that the agricultural population is unlikely to peak until after the year 2000.[12] 'Whilst this applies most accurately to Asia, the Near East and Northwest Africa, there is likely to be a deepening crises of poverty and underemployment throughout the developing world if population growth continues at its present rate'.[13] The conclusions to be drawn from this trend as regards development policy are the importance of birth control in certain areas and the need to create jobs outside agriculture (increasing the rate of industrialisation) and in agriculture (intensification of labour-based production etc.).

2. The increase of the agricultural population in absolute numbers will lead to an expansion of subsistence farming. No doubt if farmers specialise and the productivity of agricultural labour rises together with monetary income, they will be able to purchase food products and thus contribute towards the development of a market-orientated agriculture. But this process is likely to be slow and subsistence farming will certainly continue to be very important for the next few years. The educational system should not therefore neglect the subject of food crops or that of household management in rural areas. Increased supply of food products and

improvement of the standard of living of the farming community will be based on a more modern approach to food production and to household management in the rural world.

3. In view of the land area available, growth in food demand will inevitably have to be met by the introduction of *more intensive methods of farming.*

Increased agricultural production results both from extension (increased production) and intensification but, according to the IWP, intensification will account for 78 per cent of increased production in Asia and 45 per cent in Africa. In about 1985, farmers will be using almost all the area available to them in several world regions. Between 1962 and 1985 the area of cultivable land available per head of the agricultural population will drop from 0.72 to 0.56 hectares and the average available per unit of the population as a whole will drop from approximately a half to a third of a hectare. The need for intensification is therefore only too clear.

Intensification could be achieved in the following ways: by reduction of fallow and increasing the number of harvest obtained in one year from the same area, increasing the proportion of irrigated land and improving the management of water resources (flood control, drainage, etc.), increasing the purchases made by the agricultural sector (fertilisers, pesticides, animal feeding stuffs), and mechanisation and motorisation when these are economically justifiable.

4. The process of intensification, which is the basis of agricultural expansion, must be accompanied by the adjustment of production structures to those of demand. Two points are worthy of mention: the need for a breakthrough in the production of cereals and for a reduction of the protein deficit (on nutritional, hygiene and social grounds). Although protein of animal origin is to be preferred for dietetic and psychological reasons, the IWP considers that in view of the vast scale of requirements all types of protein production should be encouraged.[14]

5. Yields should be increased by improving the 'biological converters' used, i.e. the species of plants and animals raised. The IWP places great hopes on the extension of the area planted with high-yielding varieties. There is much room for improvement in the sphere of animal production, particularly as regards the selection and crossing of breeds, the improvement of animal health and animal feeding, the intensification of fodder production, etc.

2. The limitations of agricultural technology

One of the points to which the Meadows Report draws attention is the fact that 'The hopes of the technological optimists centre on the ability of technology to remove or extend the limits to growth of population and capital.'[15]

...Applying technology to the natural pressures that the environment exerts against any growth process has been so successful in the past that a whole culture has evolved around the principle of fighting against limits rather than learning to live with them. This culture has been reinforced by the apparent immensity of the earth and its resources and by the relative smallness of man and his activities.[16] ... Faith in technology as the ultimate solution to all problems can thus divert our attention from the most fundamental problem — the problem of growth in a finite system — and prevent us from taking effective action to solve it.[17]

The Meadows Report thus sounds a *warning note,* and questions a *pattern of thought which we have inherited from the past.* The essentials of the Meadows Report's approach to food production prospects can be summarised as follows:

1. In the LDCs, according to indices published by FAO, total food production rose at about the same rate as population in the 1960s: 'Thus food production *per capita* has remained nearly constant, at a low level.'[18]

2. Assuming that man's future food requirements will continue to be met by agriculture, to the extent that cultivable area is limited population growth will reduce the surface area available per inhabitant. In 1970, the world population was 3,600 million and the rate of population growth 2.1 per cent. At this rate, the world's population doubles itself in 33 years: in the year 2000 the population is thus likely to be of the order of 7,000 million.[19]

At present, the area *under cultivation* per inhabitant is of the order of 0.4 hectares (and standards of nutrition are low in the LDCs) which means a total of 1,400 million hectares under cultivation. The area which is potentially suitable for cultivation has been estimated at 3,200 million hectares, but this area is decreasing owing to urban expansion, the construction of communications networks, etc. If present rates of productivity in agriculture are maintained (0.4 hectares per person fed) and present demographic trends continue, 2,800 million hectares of agricultural land will be needed in the year 2000. Increasing amounts of money will be required to bring marginal land into use, and other sectors of activity (e.g. industry and the public sector) will also be competing for funds. '... even with the optimistic assumption that all possible land is utilised, there will still be a desperate land shortage before the year 2000 if *per capita* land requirements and population growth rates remain as they are today.'[20]

3. The 'catastrophe' could be postponed by intensifying agricultural production and increasing yields, which would reduce the surface area required to feed on person (this is an assumption of the IWP which provides for only 0.3 hectares per inhabitant). But increasing intensification will call for an increase in purchases of machines, fertilisers, pesticides, etc.

— that is, for increased consumption of other resources. Moreover, increased agricultural production may lead to deterioration of soil, pollution and the depletion of certain resources. Agricultural expansion may be limited by other factors than land, for example water supplies. Increased domestic and industrial requirements for water may reduce the amount available for agriculture. It may thus become essential to distil sea water; this is however a costly process and its use on a large scale would require more plentiful supplies of cheap energy.

Moreover, analysis of the Green Revolution shows that *the new technology must be accompanied by changes in the socio-economic conditions of production.* 'Every change in the normal way of doing things requires an adjustment time, while the population, consciously or unconsciously, restructures its social system to accommodate the change. While techology can change rapidly, political and social institutions generally change very slowly.'[21] Even if the productivity of the land can be increased fairly rapidly, limits will inevitably be reached if the population growth rate continues to be exponential. To double or quadruple the productivity of land would be to postpone the crisis for approximately thirty or sixty years respectively.[22]

4. A solution to the food problem can also be found outside agriculture. There are two possibilities: fishing and the manufacture of synthetic food. The continuous development of deep-sea fishing techniques is leading to the extinction of one ocean species after another.[23] As for synthetic food as such, at the moment it is practically non-existent.

It is obvious that if the world population increases at an exponential rate, the same should also be true of agricultural and food production. Once the process of expanding the surface area under cultivation is complete, exponential population growth implies an exponential rate of progress in farming methods.

5. Statistical analysis shows a marked inverse correlation between birth rate and *per capita* GNP. To the extent that *per capita* GNP increases, the population tends to decrease (a slight reduction in the rate of economic growth has a marked effect on the size of the population). Although many countries encourage birth control, this restrictive action cannot have any immediate effect.

3. Agricultural development and the role of education

The IWP and the Meadows Report are two basic contemporary documents of great educational value as they oblige humanity to consider the future. The many criticisms which have been levelled at them make them none the less valuable from the educational point of view; on the contrary, they offer an opportunity for deeper reflection on the future of mankind. Models of the way in which society is developing provide the generations in power with rules for action and the younger generation with an opportunity to exercise their minds on a problem which is of concern to them — the nature of the society in which they are called upon to live. An educational system which is too centred on the past will not meet the needs of the rising generations. The models furnished by the IWP and the Massachusetts Institute of Technology suggest the following considerations which are of relevance to our subject:

1. The conditions of agricultural production change as the population increases. The future may be very different from the past. If catastrophe is to be avoided, considerable attention will have to be devoted to technology. Mankind will need people who have been properly trained — as farmers, farm technicians, agronomists, etc. — and are respected members of society, aware of the importance of their role in ensuring the future of the human race;

2. Technology has its limits. More often than not it cannot be put to use without prior transformation of the socio-economic structure of society: it is in the interests of the whole of mankind to adapt the socio-economic organisation of agriculture in all countries to the need for agricultural expansion. Lastly, it is probable that logic will require population growth to be tailored to our potential, and overall economic growth to be divided between quantity and quality of life;

3. If increased production and increased productivity of labour in agriculture were to prove insufficient in the next few years, the development of the LDCs would be impossible or severely restricted. Not only would the gap between developed and less developed countries widen but the latter would move rapidly towards a catastrophe whose consequences cannot easily be foreseen;

4. Education is not of course sufficient but it is essential if the great battle against poverty, under-employment and famine is to be won. For this purpose it is necessary, however, that this struggle should be one of the avowed objectives of the educational system, which should be organised with this end in view. As far as agricultural development is concerned, it is essential to establish a system leading from creation to dissemination, what we shall call a 'creation-dissemination system', on which the development of this sector will be based.

II. THE CREATION-DISSEMINATION SYSTEM IN AGRICULTURE

1. *Definition*

We have already described the process leading from creation to dissemination as the basis for economic growth. Progress, growth and development are linked, interdependent phenomena: as the relationships between them have already been adequately described as regards both the general principles governing them and their impact on agriculture, we shall here deal more specifically with the mechanisms of agricultural progress with particular reference to LDCs. We use the term *'integrated creation-*

dissemination system' with reference to agriculture to describe a *co-ordinated* and *controlled* (in the sense of cybernetic regulation) process of research and application of research, the object of which is to adapt agriculture to the process of overall development (see Figure 1).

This process calls for the co-ordination of research centres, extension services, bodies responsible for agricultural and overall development, trade organisations and farmers.

Control is exercised in several ways. First, the new technology which has been devised in research centres must be tried out in centres which are conveniently located in relation to the different crop-growing regions or tested on 'reference farms' or 'pilot farms' before being adopted for general use. Secondly, ideas put forward at one or other stage of the creation-dissemination process must be subjected to socio-economic scrutiny with a view to determining their potential usefulness for the individual farmer and the effect they may have on agricultural growth and the socio-economic development of the nation as a whole. Lastly, the system must provide for practical evaluation (or overall assessment) of the results obtained: research workers, extension workers, farmers, intermediate technical personnel, etc., should all join in this process, and there must then be feedback machinery so that the system's design and methods can be adjusted with a view to improving its operation.

At present these two principles of coordination and control are rarely applied satisfactorily, when they are used at all. Research centres, extension services, development bodies, agricultural organisations, etc., tend to operate more or less independently and the proposals of the different bodies are not always subjected to the necessary economic scrutiny, testing, etc., before they are put into general use. Overall evaluation or assessment which results in the necessary readjustments is even rarer. The system receives directives in regard to development policy on such subjects as the medium and long-term outlook for agricultural and overall growth, the main types of production, the need to adopt more intensive methods, to step up protein production, etc. Such directives normally imply the existence of bodies drawing up long-term forecasts and plans in which the system's research workers, extension workers, etc. play their part. However, it is the duty of the political authorities to define the basic choices and priorities within the framework of the overall process of development. These may be defined at national level only (national development plan), at regional level (regional plans) or relate to specific development areas (development projects). In fact the basic political options are not always clearly defined and they may change frequently, thus making for difficulties and uncertainties at practical level.

2. The themes of extension work and agricultural production systems

The proposals of research and extension workers take the form of themes relating to specific operations (production of manure, pruning, the use of fertiliser for a particular crop, etc.), to the improvement of a type of

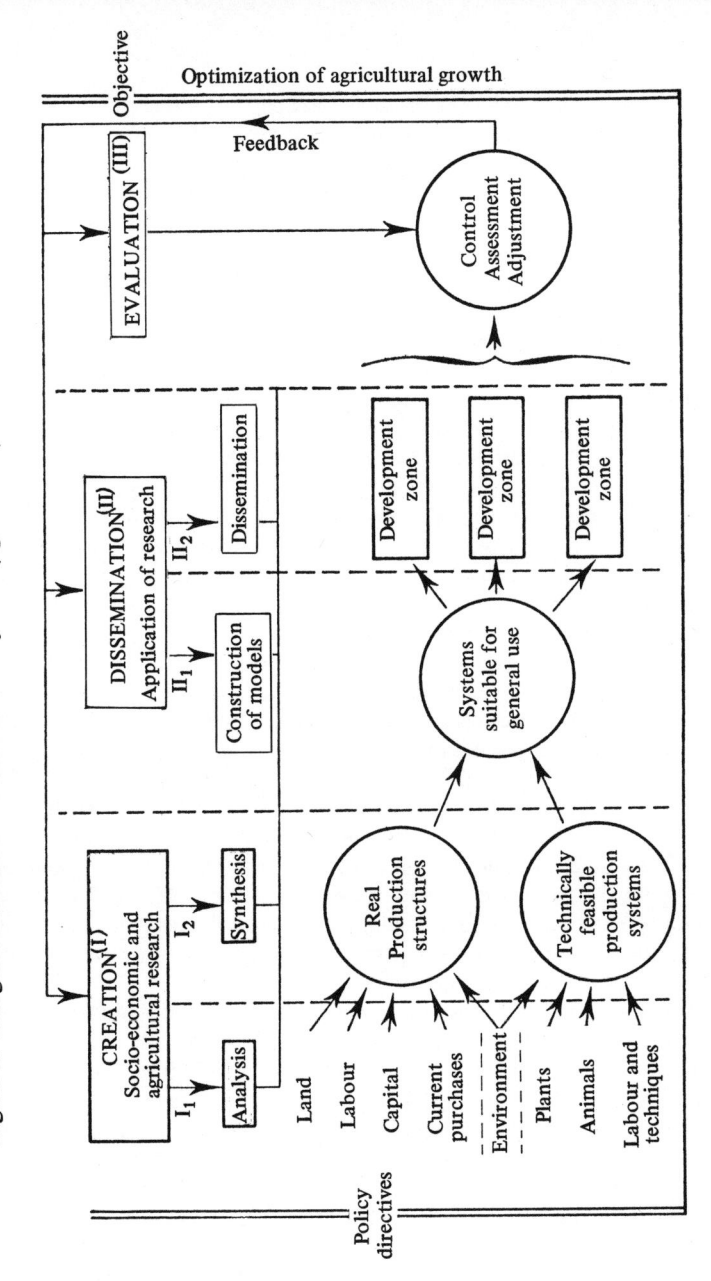

Figure 1. Integrated creation – dissemination system (agriculture)

production which involves the use of various techniques (cultivation of rice, cotton, etc.), to the introduction of an *agricultural production system* involving several different types of product, etc.

Each agricultural production system is a combination of plant and/or animal species and of methods used to raise these species. These systems may be classified in several ways, according to the nature and relative importance of the different plant and animal species raised, the extent to which they are market-orientated, the amount produced for export, the methods used (manual labour, draught animals, tractors), etc. Animal husbandry may (or may not) be integrated within the system with one or other of the five following economic functions as its main purpose: production of manure, traction, supply of products for consumption, cash reserve or capital investment. Production systems are linked with the different types of socio-economic organisation of agriculture — community (collective), freeholder (peasant) or capitalist — and must conform to certain criteria which vary in part from one type to another. If they are to make a contribution to the development of agriculture and the economy as a whole, these systems must in fact fulfil conditions which relate both to the private sector and to the economy as a whole.[24]

When the transition from subsistence agriculture to market-orientated agriculture takes place within a context of peasant farming, the first task of the production system is to meet subsistence needs, to produce a net monetary margin per working day which will serve as an incentive and ensure the system's further development, and to avoid too high a monetary capital coefficient which may involve farmers in debt. As regards their general suitability, production systems should be assessed on the basis of the value added which they produce (contribution to overall economic growth), the amount of money they put into circulation (which depends, for a given country, on the final destination of the product) and their effect on basic economic equilibria (employment, balance of payments, State budget, savings and investment).

At the different stages of the integrated creation-dissemination process, the different production systems should be assessed from the standpoint of agricultural and overall development first as possibilities, then with a view to their suitability for general use and finally in terms of the results obtained. In order to be judged suitable for general use, the systems must not only be 'possible' from the agro-economic point of view; they must also be *practicable* — which means that if an economic infrastructure does not already exist at local level, it must be possible to introduce one — and acceptable, from a socio-cultural point of view, to individuals and groups.

In most LDCs, the definition of production systems which meet the needs of development is a matter of extreme urgency. Single-crop systems orientated towards export must be diversified, a market-orientated agriculture built up on the basis of subsistence farming and plant and animal species combined in a manner compatible with agronomic requirements, the supply of manpower and socio-economic objectives. The definition and dissemination of these systems entails constant collaboration between agriculturalists, extension workers and farmers.[25]

3. Agricultural research

Measurement of the 'research ratio', i.e. expenditure on research and development as a proportion of GNP, gives a fairly clear idea of the effort made by a nation, an economic sector or a region to promote and improve knowledge. In the 1960s the United States allocated 3.4 per cent of their GNP to research and development, Western European countries as a whole 1.5 per cent and Japan 1.4 per cent. In the same way, expenditure on agro-economic research and experimentation as a proportion of agricultural GNP can serve as a pointer to the effort made to apply scientific discoveries to agriculture. In Europe in the 1960s, this proportion was highest in the Netherlands where it exceeded 1 per cent.

As the enterprises of which the agricultural sector is composed are in the main of small to medium size, the public authoritæs must take the lead in promoting agro-economic research, by stimulating joint research (within trade or mixed organisations) or by assuming complete responsibility for all aspects of research work, including organisation (specialised institutes financed wholly or almost wholly from public funds). The emergence of medium- to large-sized firms in the food industries sector makes it easier for individual firms to develop their own research departments.

In the LDCs, research institutes were established during the colonial period to serve the plantations and the export trade. Several eminent specialists have been produced by these institutions and much useful knowledge of tropical products accumulated. What usually needs to be done now is to organise (or reorganise) research services which have a better understanding of the problems of national development and to ensure consultation and co-ordination. Research stations in the LDCs should concentrate on the application of techniques and experimentation in preference to basic research: the latter can be transferred from one country to another whereas applied research (particularly with a view to devising production systems adapted to the needs of development) cannot.

While the major themes of applied research are determined by national development plans and specific geographical conditions, they will have certain common features in all LDCs, namely those deriving from long-term planning studies (intensification of agricultural production, water resources management, adaptation of technology and labour organisation, increased protein production, inclusion of fodder crops in crop rotation systems and of animal husbandry in production systems, etc.). So-called problem-based research, which brings teams of experts in different disciplines together to work on a particular problem, seems well suited to the LDCs' needs.

'Operational' agricultural research should always result in proposing production systems which meet the requirements of national agricultural development. These systems will be designed to fit into existing production structures or into new structures (land reform, creation of agro-industrial complexes, etc).

Much useful technical information often lies unused and unusable in research stations because it has not been formulated in terms of production systems. This is the main form in which technical information can be put to use by planners, project leaders and initiators and agricultural extension workers.

Developed countries for their part can make a major contribution to the battle against hunger in the LDCs by aiding agricultural research.[26] Private foundations, for example the Ford and Rockefeller Foundations, played a decisive role in development of the high-yielding varieties which were the point of departure for the Green Revolution. Most of the countries of Western Europe have established tropical research institutes and contribute towards the upkeep of large networks of research stations (France maintains a network of approximately 100 institutes which employs some 850 specialists).

The LDCs should try to make the best possible use of the capital of knowledge which has been accumulated and to extend it further. As research needs time and continuity, it can best be pursued by making a body of international experts available to States, pooling suggestions and inventions, organising regular meetings and seminars which bring together agricultural research workers from all parts of the world, developing research on a regional basis and arranging for financial assistance from developed countries. Aid for agricultural research organised with a view to accelerating growth in the LDCs is probably one of the most effective and least debatable forms of aid.

4. Collaboration between agriculturalists, economists and sociologists

The diagram of the creation-dissemination system (Figure 1) shows that the determinateon of 'production systems suitable for general use' has three stages:

1. 'Analytical' research into the basic components of production systems, both agricultural (plant and animal species, environment, etc.) and socio-economic (land, labour, capital, current purchases, etc.);
2. Formulation by agriculturalists of 'technically feasible systems' representing several alternative combinations for a given area, and depiction by economists and sociologists of the socio-economic structures actually existing in that area;
3. By comparing these technically feasible systems and existing structures, determination of socio-economic approaches and models suitable for general use.

The aim of this creation-dissemination system is to arrange for continuous collaboration between agriculturalists, agro-economists and agro-sociologists on a much more satisfactory basis than at present. It is not really possible to formulate valid technical solutions without a thorough knowledge not only of the physical surroundings but also of the human environment, the forms of socio-economic organisation of production, and their capacity for change, and the factors which may hold back or block progress.

From the point of view of their operation, actual socio-economic systems can be described in terms of specific production relationships which involve a main decision-making centre and one or more secondary decision-making centres and usually combine several different production systems (arable farming and animal husbandry). This general definition can be easily applied to analysis even of such complex socio-economic units as the 'carre sénégalais'[27] or others of similar type. Although the different forms of socio-economic organisation in agriculture have been the subject of considerable research, it must be admitted that the studies produced so far are rarely concerned with the operational side and that much still remains to be done to define methods of survey and analysis that would make it possible to describe – and possibly establish a typology of – actual socio-economic forms of organisation which could be used as a basis for the process of dissemination. For the aim is not only to explain situations but to change them – and such changes generally come about as a result of inter-disciplinary action.

When planning growth and development, it is particularly important to assess actual or potential supplies of land, manpower and, possibly, capital. Studies of the labour situation (days available, jobs to be done, techniques used) should be prepared both at the research stations (standards) and on the spot (manpower available and assessment of underemployment).

Simultaneous research into *technically feasible systems* and *actual production structures* will provide the basic information *for the construction of systems which can be put into general use.* Models constructed should allow for the heterogeneity of structures and, for each type of structure proposed, should offer farmers some degree of choice. Budgeting and planning methods may be used to determine standard reference models. All the information available should be used in the determination of systems suitable for general use, a process in which the personnel of research bureaux and institutes, extension workers, farmers' representatives and, wherever possible, farmers themselves, should all take part. It is indeed essential that farmers or their genuine representatives should be involved in the search for new systems to replace existing ones and the support of those whom it most closely concerns be enlisted for the dissemination campaign. More generally, the support of all bodies and persons concerned must be obtained and objectives, methods, means and roles clearly defined.

5. Networks for the propagation and dissemination of progress

Invention, experimentation, demonstration, participation of 'pioneer' farmers willing to use the new techniques and dissemination at village community level are the successive stages of agricultural progress. The process may be organised by commercial networks (food and agricultural industries), by trade organisations or by public authorities. Most of the countries of Western Europe began to organise 'extension services' at the end of the nineteenth century, intensifying and amplifying them during the twentieth. The Netherlands have the highest density of extension workers (approximately 200 farms, 500 workers and 2,000 hectares per extension worker), followed by Denmark with 250 farms per extension worker. The scope of agricultural extension work has gradually been widened: at first limited to the technical aspects of production, it gradually became more and more concerned with the scientific organisation of work, farm management, marketing, household management, etc. Alongside the official networks large firms producing agricultural machinery, fertilisers, pesticides, animal feeding stuffs, etc. launched marketing services whose publicity was designed to appeal to farmers and keep them informed of the latest developments. As agriculture-based food industries developed and contractual relationships were formed between food firms and agricultural establishments, the 'integration contract' generally included technical clauses designed to ensure rapid and controlled dissemination of technical information in accordance with market requirements.

Most LDCs nowadays also have extension services. These have a decisive role to play in the process of agricultural growth, their threefold tasks being:

(a) to keep farmers up to date and help in the process of innovation by establishing machinery which will involve the farmers themselves in this process;
(b) with the aid of specialised departments, to assist in functional training, whether in the sphere of literacy work (enabling farmers to read invoices, weigh their produce, calculate their income, etc.), or in regard to health (for farming techniques which require that the whole of the farmer's family be in good health), nutrition (use of food crops), standard of living (use of monetary income) and way of life (planning of work). Although such functional training may appear insufficient, its importance should not be underestimated and it may encourage an interest in acquiring a more comprehensive training;
(c) to detect the 'real leaders' (not always identical with the official leaders) who will be able to ensure that their group is genuinely in favour of development operations agreed to, and will also be able to assume responsibility in farmers' organisations, particularly in co-operatives.

Most LDCs are now aware of the crucial importance of an agricultural extension network but the energy with which the policy is pursued varies considerably from one country to another, as can be seen by reference to numbers of farming households per extension worker. In 1971, the ratio was almost 15,000 to one in Guatemala, 8,000 to one in Mali and Bolivia, 2,000 to one in Venezuela and Senegal, and between 800 and 1,000 to one in Chile, Zambia and India.[28] But this is only a very rough indication: the significance of these figures depends on such factors as geographical dispersion, means of communication and transport available to the extension worker, the objectives pursued, the actual responsibilities of the extension worker (administrative role), the methods used, etc.

6. Methods used in extension work

There would appear to be two basic approaches to training and information for rural development, which could be termed respectively the 'under supervision' approach and the 'community development' approach. The main characteristic of the 'under supervision' approach is the fact that the methods disseminated by the extension services are *'tried and tested'*. This type of service may be organised by the Ministry of Agriculture, by development corporations, or in connection with specific development projects. The initiative is taken by bodies which have *experimented* with the techniques (experimental plots) and, having *proved* their effectiveness (demonstration plots), are certain that their dissemination will contribute towards progress. The process of dissemination is then undertaken more often than not by a professional hierarchy — people with degrees in agricultural science or farm management, aided by field instructors and extension workers. Bearing in mind the objectives and intensity of the extension work, it is even possible to define different types of structures within the 'under supervision' approach, distinguishing between them on the basis of the differing ratios of one category of supervisory staff to another.

The 'under supervision' approach is sometimes reminiscent of the methods used in colonial times, often taking the form of 'directives' to which the farmer submits rather than accepting them of his own free will. The dissemination of new techniques can only be said to be successful if they continue to be applied after the supervisory staff have gone home and, in some cases, when certain advantages have been withdrawn. There are many examples of reversion to the *status quo ante* once the launching campaign is over, the only difference — unfortunately — being deep mistrust of further attempts at innovation. But it is also possible to quote examples of success, particularly with regard to specific operations (production of manure, use of fertiliser, improvement of animal feeding, etc.), or even operations concerned with a particular product (cultivation of rice, ground-nuts, maize, etc.).

Successful campaigns are based more often than not on preliminary tests and controls on extension services which have a clear understanding of their role and on methods which associate farmers as much as possible in the action undertaken, using patient demonstration and persuasion. Although criticism has been levelled at the 'under supervision' approach to agricultural extension work, its methods can and should be improved. One should not underestimate the role which this type of approach can play in improving productivity and increasing the agricultural surplus during the take-off period and for as long as levels of training and information in agriculture do not make it possible to use other methods as a basis for agricultural growth. Dissemination of information by agricultural extension services played an important part in the agricultural growth of the West.

The 'under supervision' approach is much less likely to be effective, however, when radical changes are to be made in production systems (new crop rotations, including the introduction of fodder crops into the rotation system, the incorporation of animal husbandry, schemes for land improvement, irrigation, etc.). Such radical changes threaten traditional socio-economic structures and more often than not require certain preliminary conditions to be met (land reform, organisation of distribution networks and credit, etc.), raising genuine development problems rather than short-term economic growth problems. As for community development, the corresponding French term *animation* has been defined by Yves Goussault as 'a special form of education, directly connected with the introduction of new structures for rural development, which concerns all categories of the population involved in these programmes, farmers and supervisory staff alike.'[29] The term 'animation' has long been accepted in French-speaking countries; it corresponds fairly closely to the English term 'community development' and the term 'promoción' used in Latin America By this definition, community development or 'animation' therefore takes into account all the different aspects of development: technical, economic, sociological and political. Its aim is to train men to play their part in society, to take initiative and make decisions. It may form part of the central government machinery (community development planning) or come under land reform programmes or the activities of bodies involved in development at local level. The aim here is not simply to produce more rice or meat but rather to provide agricultural and civic education for the rural community and to establish co-operatives and other institutions to promote long-term rural development, institutions for which the farmers themselves must be capable of assuming responsibility. Seen from this angle the dissemination of new techniques is a result of farmer participation and, ultimately, of decisions taken by rural communities. Extension services, therefore cease to be directive and become more in the nature of advisory.

This type of action accordingly falls fully within the concept of development, particularly if development is defined as the way in which social groups envisage their future and the means which they feel must be used to achieve such a future. It is much more than dissemination of techniques, conducive though it is to the development and application of an an innovative approach in general.

Community development is more ambitious than a technical extension service; it encounters opposition from several quarters (a multiplicity of traditional centres of power), can only be successful if requested by the appropriate authorities, requires accurate assessment of what is feasible, etc Indeed, the 'community development' approach may be very slow to affec technical progress for many reasons — the inhibiting effect of tensions aroused within a heterogeneous social fabric, the slowness of psycho-social mechanisms and of the transformations which are a prerequisite for growth, the difficulty of organising close collaboration between rural development services and the technical extension services, etc.

The disastrous effects of compartmentalisation and differences of approach sometimes due to different backgrounds, training, etc. should not be underestimated. Of course, the aim is to produce *as soon as possible* people fully equipped to play their part as farmers and citizens, but calories and proteins must be produced *now* and to do this methods and objectives must be adapted to the different stages of the development process.

The answer is not to oppose the 'under supervision' and the 'community development' approaches but to replace the former by the latter as soon as possible, or rather to combine them in a single whole. Of course, the technical extension services may wish to hold the reins as long as possible, in which case a technocratic approach may prevent the farmers from playing a full part as soon as they might. On the other hand, community development services may tend to underestimate the importance of technology, as regards both training and operations. A basic conclusion we have reached is that *what must be striven for simultaneously is both willingness to accept change and the means to achieve it.* In the field which concerns us, change implies technical competence. This means that community development workers and agricultural extension workers must be able to form *operational teams* or, failing that, that community development workers must acquire technical expertise and the technical experts some knowledge of sociology.

7. Evaluation of propagation-dissemination systems

Evaluation is of great importance as it is the basis for improving or reshaping the system. All those who have contributed towards the final result, whether research workers, extension workers, administrators, farmers or representatives of professional bodies, should take part in its evaluation. Inadequacies likely to emerge are:

1. Irrelevance of applied agricultural research to development objectives or the need for further investigation of certain themes, modification of the proposed system, etc.;
2. Failure of socio-economic research to detect factors likely to hold back or block development or to define the socio-economic conditions which must exist before new systems can be introduced, giving an inadequate or inaccurate picture of the actual structures, passing over inadequacies in distribution networks and credit facilities, etc.;
3. Lack of communication between agricultural and socio-economic research workers, making it impossible to define realistic systems suitable for general use, evaluated in terms of the benefit derived from them both by the individual and by society in general;
4. Inefficiency of the extension services, either due to having

overestimated farmers' receptiveness and the role of agricultural organisations (in particular co-operatives) or to the use of unsatisfactory techniques (the 'under supervision' or 'community development' approach) or to insufficient training and information, bearing in mind the difficulties inherent in the themes or systems which have to be got across;
5. Delays caused by administrative red tape or inability of the departments concerned to ensure supplies of raw materials, equipment and spare parts or the marketing of products;
6. Farmers' reluctance or refusal to co-operate, for reasons which should be carefully ascertained.

This is not an exhaustive list. Similar lists could be drawn up by bodies or departments specialising in project evaluation but the results must be made known to all those involved and, if appropriate, used as a basis for 'round table' discussions in which different views can be compared and decisions reached on the changes which should be made to the development process.

Such procedures are rarely applied; they come up against the traditional compartmentalisation between different bodies although all are supposed to be promoting development, not to mention personal and interinstitutional rivalries, interdepartmental wrangling, etc. The true promoters of development are in the last analysis those who show an ability to lead groups defined in terms of specific objectives. To develop is to learn how to work together.

8. Real and apparent adoption of new systems

The results of the creation-dissemination process can be measured in terms of the *real adoption* of new systems, that is to say the extent to which use of the new technology is continued or extended after the disappearance of certain temporary advantages (bonuses, subsidies for the purchase of certain products, advantageous sales terms, compensation for certain working days, etc.) which encourage *apparent adoption* of the new techniques. When farmers are genuinely convinced of their usefulness, the new methods and structures are definitively adopted and a permanent increase in the productivity of land and, it is to be hoped, of labour should result. Moreover these innovations can be the beginning of a cumulative process, creating new requirements and assisting in the creation of a progressive society.

What it comes down to is this, that *the farmer must be brought into the creation-dissemination process in two ways: in the first place, innovations must be in response to his prompting; secondly, he must be enabled to participate in the relevant decisions.* Too many mistakes have been made by experts, specialists, development corporations, government departments, etc. for the blame for slow agricultural development to be laid solely at the door of the farmer. It is also caused by mistakes made by services which exist to help the farmers, whose suspicion of them is often justified.

Real adoption implies in the first place a possibility of technical and economic success. For example, before encouraging farmers to use fertilisers, it is usually necessary to get them to plant crops in rows, a technique which makes for much more rapid weeding. If it is to lead to the desired results, technical extension work must necessarily pay heed to the logical time sequence of projected operations. Economic success means an *increase in the farmer's monetary income,* hence increased purchasing power which will enable him to raise his standard of living and continue the process of agricultural modernisation. So far, the effect of new techniques on the monetary income of farmers has not, generally speaking, been thoroughly enough investigated, though new systems proposed are known to have sometimes involved the farmer in debt. It is therefore essential to provide machinery whereby studies can be undertaken which will clarify the position in this respect.

Lastly, if the farmer's genuine acceptance of new methods is to be ensured, his problems must be understood, his dignity respected and his motives ascertained. The experience and adaptability of the farmer are often underestimated by specialists raised in an urban environment, saturated with too general an education, unskilled in observing and grasping practical situations and — even more serious — sometimes too conscious of their superiority and even condescending towards the farmer. It can be taken as axiomatic that it is difficult to help a man without trying to understand him and without a deep respect for his personality.

Those responsible for development can make suggestions which are perfectly reasonable and logical from their point of view but farmers will not accept them if they do not conform with their logic. For example, in the LDCs it is difficult to encourage a type of product which seems a profitable proposition in general terms if it does not guarantee the food requirements of the farmer's family. In many parts of the world, this means that rice must be grown as a subsistence crop before any other type of product can be considered. Areas favourable for rice growing should therefore be reserved first and foremost for this crop and for its improvement. Once the farmer is sure that he can provide his family with the amount of rice necessary for its subsistence, he will be more likely to accept other proposals.

Lastly, what counts is the support of a social group, not that of a few individuals. In the LDCs, the individual is generally subject to strong pressure from the social group. This means that those responsible for development must be familiar with local customs and traditions. The group will contain 'real leaders' who will not always be the official leaders (local representatives of external services). The failure of pilot farm systems, show farms, etc. can often be explained by an unwise choice of an individual farmer. The farmer chosen may in any case be considered a social deviant by the group if the latter was not already in agreement. Hence the importance of the community development approach, to the extent that it makes it possible to identify the group's real representatives.[30]

9. Participation of the rural world in the effects of economic growth

The integration of the rural world in the development process should not be seen only in terms of the rural world's contribution towards economic growth, but also in terms of *its share in the benefits of such growth.* Available statistics show that, in general, agriculture's share of GDP is much lower than its share of the total population. GDP per unit of the agricultural population is often only 50 to 60 per cent of GDP per unit of the population as a whole and, rather than improving in recent years, this state of affairs has often worsened. Although these figures are rough approximations, there are many other indications which confirm the relatively low level of agricultural incomes. However, disparity between the rural and the urban world is not to be measured only in terms of income. Many other factors are involved, including inequality in public spending (on schools, hospitals, electricity, water, etc.). These disparities in private income and public spending lead to serious inequalities for young people as far as access to better jobs is concerned, particularly through education. Several explanations can be found for the low level of farm incomes in relation to incomes generally: the relatively low productivity of labour, the fact that part of the profit on increased productivity is transferred to the pockets of dominant social groups, cheap food policies, State levies distributed in accordance with the development policy adopted, etc.

At the beginning of the development process, the effects on the standard of living in rural areas may filter through very slowly, but if this state of affairs continues, it will give rise to serious political problems. Poverty will drive the rural population to the towns in a swelling, insensate flood which strains urban reception capacity to and beyond the limit; low monetary incomes will not encourage the extension or intensification of agricultural production, and the agricultural investment which is essential to ensure continuing growth will be impossible. If farm incomes are low, farmers will be unable to purchase industrial products: industrial growth, which is more often than not based on expansion of the internal market, could thus be held back or blocked. Low economic growth in the agricultural sector can also lead to a drop in exports, hence to increased demand for imported foodstuffs and a reduced capacity to purchase capital goods. If rural incomes are kept low over a long period, widespread discontent in country areas and blockage of economic growth will be the inevitable result.

CHAPTER 3. INTEGRATION OF THE RURAL WORLD INTO THE OVER-ALL EDUCATIONAL SYSTEM

1. 'Ruralisation' of the overall educational system

When one remembers that the rural world is a fundamental factor in many countries, that mankind will need to achieve an unprecedented breakthrough in agricultural development in the next few years in order to meet increased food requirements and ensure its survival and that agricultural development and the improvement of the productivity of farm labour are the basis on which a new society can be built, it seems clear that one of the aims of the educational system as a whole should be to make all citizens aware of the importance of the rural world and of agricultural labour in evolving societies and to inculcate a respect for manual labour and for nature. In fact, analysis of the present situation shows that the so-called 'general' education courses have little to say about the battle against hunger and the role of agriculture in the overall development process — a process which is itself given scant attention in general courses when it is not completely ignored.

The LDCs have adopted Western education which produces 'educated men' but Western culture itself emerged in a society where available resources and technological progress created the illusion that there were no limits to growth. However, the situation has changed. Models for evolving societies cannot be determined by extrapolating historical models. The population explosion, the depletion of natural resources and the deterioration of the natural environment have created a new situation which evolving societies must take into account. Young people should be trained by a new kind of general education to face the problems of their present and future.

The concept of an agriculture in decline where agricultural development is achieved by uneducated 'peasants' is one which the LDCs have inherited from the West and which no longer corresponds to the realities of their situation. The task confronting them is one of Herculean dimension: the whole population must be made aware of the problems facing them and all citizens given the broadest possible training in regard to the mechanism of socio-economic development.

2. The integration of rural and agricultural education into the overall educational system

The need for agricultural development on an unprecedented scale calls for an unprecedented development of education in the rural world. The authors of the IWP write:

> With very few exceptions in the countries studied, trained manpower for the essential agricultural services will, either quantitatively or qualitatively, and often in both respects, be a major constraint on

agricultural development. This is a recurrent theme of all the technical chapters of the plan and is amply confirmed by the specific study of the subject in the manpower chapter. There is, therefore, an unprecedented training problem associated with agricultural progress in the developing countries. At the corresponding stage of their own advancement, none of the present developed countries had to face problems of the same magnitude.[1]

The rural world will need competent and dynamic leaders if it is to win the battle against hunger and succeed in a policy for agricultural development. We know, however, that this can only be achieved on condition that the modernisation of agriculture is accompanied by development of rural education and also on condition that rural education is not seen as an inferior brand, condemning those who pass through it to live in a cultural ghetto for the rest of their lives.

The standard of education in the rural world and progress with the modernisation of agriculture are closely connected. Young graduates in the United States can find many opportunities, both in organisations and departments connected with agriculture and food in agriculture itself, to deploy their talents and develop their personalities. In Europe, more and more young farmers are receiving a sound training and high-quality technical instruction and many short training and information courses are organised for their benefit. But an archaic or traditional agricultural system has no place for people with training. More than training is necessary for development; those who have been trained must be able to find a suitable place in the socio-economic structures of the country. We are in full agreement with F.H. Harbison when he writes

> In this age of rising aspirations and spreading mass communication, the sons of farmers are not going to sentence themselves to traditional agriculture if they can possibly avoid it. The only fundamental solution is the modernisation of rural life. This calls for sweeping measures such as land reform, agricultural research and extension services, widespread rural community development programmes, the effective utilisation of rural labour in the building of roads, irrigation systems, houses, and schools, and other programmes aimed at making rural life more productive and attractive. If people see a positive reason for remaining in the rural areas and a promise of a better life there, the problem of revision of curricula in the schools will be relatively easy to handle.[2]

If the modernisation of rural life does not keep step with the development of education, the flight from the land will inevitably be accelerated as escape from the rural environment is seen as the only way of putting the education one has acquired to good use. In Europe, during the last two centuries, farmers have complained that the best of their number were being 'creamed off' the countryside. But obviously no sector of activity can hope to keep the 'cream' if it does not offer them opportunities to use their knowledge and scoope for their energy as well as a life-style which measures up to their personal aspirations. There is a clear relationship between standard of education and level of economic activity in a given sector.

When faced with the fact that against a background of traditional agriculture training tends to accelerate the flight from the land, some draw the conclusion that education should be related more specifically to the rural environment. This is the view of those for whom education is a privileged variable able to act independently of the real socio-economic context. But all good schools will encourage the child to look beyond his own immediate horizons, and any man who has received a good education will seek to improve his standard and style of life and to develop his personality by making optimum use of his knowledge and of his capacity to learn and act. The 'ruralisation' of education may result in curricula and qualifications which are not recognised as equivalent to those of general education and make it difficult or impossible for the country child to go on from 'rural education' to higher education, at the same time denying him the chance to switch over to general education in mid-stream. There have even been cases of refusal to issue diplomas in case they should be officially considered as valid for non-agricultural activity! In such cases, agricultural education is not a 'sub-system' of the overall education system but a ghetto, a closed system: let no-one be surprised therefore if those who enter it do so either because they are unaware of the real situation or because they have no choice!

The problems of rural development cannot be solved by educational segregation. If the 'ruralisation' of education were to make access to secondary schools more difficult, the farming community would interpret it as social segregation and would be less and less willing to accept it. They are already becoming more critical, and with good reason, of the obstacles their children have to overcome when they seek jobs in the town or administrative posts, particularly when, in a traditional agricultural context, the possibility of escape afforded by education appears to be the only way of improving one's social position and one's standard and style of living. If the flight from the countryside to the towns is to be halted, the socio-economic structures of agriculture must be transformed and the relative positions of the country- and the town-dweller modified. But better information services will also be needed to counter more effectively the pathological urge to get away from the land, the illusory attractions of the town and the unemployment of trained minds.

Educational segregation is no answer to the problems of the flight from the land; rural education can only be given its true significance by objective information and the modernisation of agriculture. The clear-sighted, resourceful and properly trained people whom humanity needs to overcome the looming threat of famine will not be attracted by narrow, specialised diplomas but by the opportunity to develop their personalities and use their

ies to the full. What are needed are people with a sound
ral-cum-technical education, who are aware of the importance of their role in evolving societies and whose earnings are commensurate with the part they actually play in the socio-economic development of their country. This will generally entail on the one hand a revision of the civil service system of grading, with its traditional respect for general education or for Western models based on complicated entrance examinations relating to Western socio-cultural contexts, and on the other hand special rewards for people who choose to work 'in the field' thereby forfeiting the comforts and conveniences of those who work in city offices.

The basic problem does not seem to be that of the establishment of a specifically agricultural education but rather that of training men who will work together to achieve their country's development; the question is therefore rather one of integrating rural education and creating a new overall educational system. This does not mean that education in an agricultural and rural environment should not differ in any respect from education in other contexts; however, the difference should not be defined *a priori* (which would leave too much scope for prejudice) but only after the system as a whole has been elaborated; the specific nature of agricultural and rural education should have a functional basis and not serve the purpose of segregation or social rigidity. Our first concern will therefore be to consider the basic educational principles which should apply to all citizens, whether country- or town-dwellers, on the understanding that application of these principles to all may involve adjustment of the educational system to specific contexts (the rural environment, race or ethnic group, aptitude, etc.).

Although our aim is to introduce an overall educational system of which the rural world will form part, we realise that the integration of the rural world will take time and will necessarily go hand in hand with the process of socio-economic development. We must therefore allow for a transitional period and define its characteristics. Our view of how socio-economic development should proceed, overall and in agriculture, necessarily leads us, however, to a view as to how education should develop, overall and in the rural world, guiding us towards an institutional and qualitative type of planning as opposed to straightforward quantitative expansion, whether planned or not.

I. THE BASIC PRINCIPLES OF THE EDUCATIONAL SYSTEM

1. The overall educational system

We have already touched on the question of the concept of an overall educational system and defined its content (Chapter 1, Section II, B,1). We have said that it concerns the whole population of a given country, that it may affect the individual at any period of his life and that it is composed of interdependent and co-ordinated sub-systems: the school and university sub-system, basic education for adults and further training for adults or life-long education in the true sense of the world. The overall educational system is the foundation upon which the creation-dissemination system (Chapter 1, Section I, B,2), the instrument of a progressive society, is built. The development of a creation-dissemination system involves expenditure, the distribution of which between training, research and information is one of the basic characteristics of strategy in the field of 'intellectual investment' (Chapter 1, Section II, B,3).

By the term overall system we mean, in the first place, a system for the whole population, that is to say, one which is designed to prevent educational segregation on the basis of social origin or the educational stream chosen. The system is built to allow for vertical movement (progress from one level to the next) and horizontal movement (change of stream) and has no place for 'road closed', 'one way street' or 'no through road' signs. The education of all citizens is based on the same principles and all will eventually achieve complete equality of opportunity (this point will be dealt with in the following sub-section). This cannot be said to be the case when the educational stream or ladder is decided on once and for all at the end of the primary stage (largely on the basis of social background), when certain courses or streams are unrelated to the 'common core' (or general syllabus), when change of stream during schooling is impossible (lack of 'bridge classes', non-equivalence of diplomas), and when access to certain levels of training is practically closed to those who have followed a certain course. In such circumstances, we may speak of the coexistence of closed systems but not of an overall system containing within it co-ordinated and interdependent sub-systems.

A functional overall system provides a basic training which is the same for all pupils for as long as possible and yet prepares them for the different responsibilities which must be assumed in a developing society. For example, after a common basic training, diversification may begin in the top classes of school, of adult courses or of multi-purpose educational institutions. The system will at the very least provide 'bridge classes' and offer the widest possible choice of course and opportunities for changing course in accordance with the process of development and personal aspirations.

An overall system must necessarily provide for diversity as it is training its pupils to assume different roles in society, but what counts in the last analysis are the rules and regulations which govern this diversity. Curricula and methods need not necessarily be identical just because the end in view is the same: different ways may be chosen in order to encourage the ability to express oneself and take action. Indeed, there is no need for identity of methods and curricula even for equivalent training courses: one country contains many ethnic groups, many languages and many social groupings. Equality of opportunity is not provided by the 'single school' but rather by adapting content and methods to the socio-economic contexts which have conditioned ability and outlook. Educational strategy must therefore be decentralised and diversified. The overall educational system must not only be all-embracing and democratic in order to serve the whole population: it must also be able to come into operation at any time in the life of the individual.

Not only in order to achieve maximum technical, economic and educational effectiveness but also for reasons based on social justice and humanity, life-long education is now becoming the foundation stone upon which the overall educational system, including of course the sub-systems which compose it, is built (Introduction, 5). Implementation of the principle of life-long education leads to a redistribution of funds and of teaching in space and time.[3] It leads to the diversification, the deformalisation (one might even say the desacralisation) of educational institutions: what counts in the last analysis is not the academic career individual has followed but his ability at a given moment in time.[4] What must therefore be done is to replace the present conception of full-time training during 'schooling' by the concept of a linked chain of educational experiences acquired in the course of one's working life.

Introduction of the principle of life-long education makes it imperative to re-think the objectives, the methods and the instruments of the sub-systems belonging to the overall system, and to see their interdependence, their co-ordination and their relative importance in a new light. However, ability to choose the right course of action and to justify it is not only determined by the structure of the educational system and its effectiveness: it is also determined by the whole socio-economic context. Education is also provided by the family, by social groups (youth movements, professional organisations, political parties, etc.), by the content and forms of thought and action projected by the mass media (press, radio, cinema, television), by the different forms of socio-economic organisation and the way in which they are run (hierarchical structure, participation, joint management, etc.), by the actual workings of political democracy, etc. Beyond the institutionalised overall educational system, that ambitious project the 'learning society' is beginning to emerge.[5]

2. *Equality of opportunity*

Available statistics show that access to education varies widely according to country, ethnic group and race, sex, urban or rural area, social grouping, etc. Equality of opportunity is much in evidence as a slogan but difficult to find in practice. In such circumstances, declarations regarding educational democracy appear to many as 'hypocrisy . . . the use of a smoke screen of pseudo-democratic phrases to cloak real injustice'.[6]

Inequality of educational opportunity reflects social inequality, disparities in nutrition, hygiene and medical care, life-style, the educational background of parents, etc. It is the product of society in the first place but it may either be maintained by an educational system which is used as an instrument for perpetuating the *status quo,* or be reduced by an educational system which helps to provide a greater measure of democracy.
Segregational systems which direct young people towards either general or

technical education at a very early age, offering no possibility of choice or change of course thereafter, and do not adapt training to specific contexts (ethnic group, area, etc.) in fact increase inequality of opportunity both at entrance to and exit from the different stages of the system.

Country children are among the least privileged as regards access to education and the rural world will therefore inevitably show great interest in any measure which is designed to increase equality of opportunity. However, the struggle to achieve complete equality of opportunity will be long and arduous: it has not been completed even in the most advanced countries and university education is still a very long-term objective in the LDCs.

On behalf of the developed countries, the OECD's Centre for Educational Research and Innovation asked Professor Torsten Husén to draw up a report on the ways in which equality of opportunity could be increased.[7] The Husen Report proposes three types of measure:

1. The extension of pre-school education;
2. The reform of educational institutions;
3. Life-long education.

The role of the pre-school period and of social background in early childhood in determining cultural assets has been recognised for many years. Pre-school education is thus one way of increasing equality of opportunity but it can accentuate inequalities if it is only offered to those who are already privileged. In advanced countries, the town is better provided with such services than the country and in the LDCs, where full attendance at primary schools has still not been achieved, it would be idle to hope for this type of education to be provided in rural areas and consequently to place any faith in pre-school education as a means of reducing inequality of opportunity.

The reform of educational institutions must affect structures and methods. Traditional measures, which include the provision of free education, scholarships, student hostels, etc., which all represent considerable progress towards greater social justice, are not enough.[8] Premature choice and selection must be abolished together with all forms of educational segregation. When selection is necessary, it should take place at the latest possible stage. 'The more flexible the system, i.e. the longer the options are kept open, the higher the degree of equity.'[9] T. Husén goes so far as to propose that training and the examinations which give access to a career should be dissociated. 'The school should teach while society should examine.'[10]

All things considered, life-long education offers the best prospect of establishing equality of opportunity and may be able to counteract the dominance of school which can decide the course of a whole life by success or failure in examinations.[11] 'Once education becomes continual, ideas as to what constitutes success and failure will change. An individual who fails at a given age and level in the course of his educational career will have other opportunities. He will no longer be relegated for life to the ghetto of his own failure.'[12] Life-long education will also make it possible for an individual to switch careers, whether this is necessitated by economic growth or by new or higher aspirations in the individual or group.

In the LDCs the reorganisation of educational institutions with a view to ensuring more equality of opportunity will not be easy for various reasons: the younger nations cannot meet the cost of mass education and must train the personnel they need as rapidly as possible, using schools inherited from colonial times, providing short vocational courses, etc. There is in fact a danger that the promotion of social equality will be sacrificed to the urgent requirements of economic effectiveness. The LDCs could however make much more use of life-long education and other means of self-improvement than they have done in the past. Particular attention should be paid to the establishment of centres for such purposes. These should be the educational institutions for young developing nations as much if not more than schools and universities, whose structures, methods and curricula are often too deeply influenced by the past and Western models.

3. Teaching methods which reflect blueprints for society

Educational systems cannot escape the general process of creative destruction. They must undergo reform or radical change as new discoveries and inventions are made in the field of the basic sciences (biology, psychology, linguistics, anthropology, cybernetics, etc.), of the applied sciences (operational research, systems analysis, teaching methods, etc.) and of techology (audio-visual equipment, mass media, computer techniques, etc.) and as new approaches are evolved in the light of teaching experience (functional literacy training, adult education, non-directive teaching, group techniques, etc.).[13]

Curiously enough, although the educational sector is normally one of the largest sectors of activity, its expenditure on research and development does not correspond to its size. Research into teaching methods is, however, essential if educational systems are to be renewed and adapted; the establishment of experimental institutions should also be made a priority. Changes in teaching methods are not always derived from scientific discoveries, technological inventions and new approaches to teaching practice: they can also be dictated by social change and new blueprints for society.

Teaching methods used in the West are to a large extent the result of the social conditions prevailing in the nineteenth century, which means an emphasis on individualism (individual rewards and penalties for individual work), egalitarianism (a single school system, with centralised education identical in content and methods throughout the country), hierarchical organisation (teacher-pupil relationships, directive teaching, etc.) and so on. Teaching methods, which are one aspect of the educational system, are, like the system itself, the product of a given society, but they can also help to encourage new social relationships in accordance with new blueprints for society.

A society which wishes to promote genuine democracy encourages its young people to assume their responsibilities at an early age and relates education to specific contexts, decentralising it, distributing it in space and time and eventually introducing teaching methods which are neither directive nor institutional.[14] A society which aims to develop community structures should encourage team-work at school, using group techniques,[15] self-management and co-management.[16] A society which wishes to introduce mass education in order to ease social relationships, organise equality of opportunity and achieve the most rapid rate of development possible should diversify access routes to the different levels of training and make full use of educational technology, in particular the mass media (films, video-cassettes, radio, conventional or cable television, computers). Experiments using educational radio and television services have shown that the use of mass media does present difficulties and that there are as yet few people with the specialised training enabling them to use these instruments effectively. Experiments carried out so far would seem to favour multi-media programmes, which combine television, radio, the press, correspondence courses, group meetings in community centres, etc. In the LDCs, lack of equipment, particularly as regards television sets, can also be a problem. In North America, there are more radio sets than people while in Africa and South Asia there are only 45 and 33 sets respectively per thousand inhabitants. Of the 250 million television sets in the world, fewer than 5 million are to be found in Africa, South Asia and the Arab States.[17]

Diversification of educational institutions and the expansion of the different forms of adult education have created a new educational 'market' and call for a new approach to curriculum content and teaching methods. Modern teaching methods must be related to a wider framework than that of the school and must seek to serve the needs of life-long, nation-wide education.

Several new methods have been pioneered in adult education: group methods, adjustment of courses to the environment and individual needs, non-directive, non-institutional methods, widespread use of audio-visual aids, etc. These new approaches have tended to have a marked effect on pupil/teacher relationships, on the role of the teacher (diagnosis of pupil needs and motives, group planning of curricula, etc.), on methods used (technological aids, formulation of textbooks, models, etc.) and on evaluation procedures, which are applied not only to the pupils but to teachers and institutions as well. The idea is gaining ground that teachers should operate in teams which include both permanent and visiting members (teachers 'on loan' from other schools or who normally fulfil other functions in society).

These trends should bring about a radical transformation of teacher training courses which could best be described by saying that, instead of training students to teach a particular subject, we should be aiming more and more to train 'educators' in the full sense of the word. Such training entails consideration of the aims of education in relation to socio-economic development, a thorough knowledge of teaching methods and the scientific discoveries on which they are based, not to mention the human relationships involved, and great flexibility on the part of the teacher, for contrary to the tradition that the learner bows to rules pre-ordained by the teaching system, it is the teacher who should adapt himself to the learner.[18]

The way in which knowledge is handed down, which depends basically on the teaching methods employed, is thus both the product of past social relationships and a foretaste of new ones, either in relation to society's blueprints for the future or by virtue of the educational system's own, independent capacity for innovation.

4. Learning to be . . . agents of development

Victory in the world drive to achieve the basic objectives of the human economy — to provide food, training, information, medical care and accommodation, to improve the quality of life, to preserve or renew natural resources, etc. — calls for mobilisation of all man's intelligence and energy.

Development can be achieved in many ways, depending on historical and geographic processes and contexts and on the prevailing socio-political philosophy, but it is the main problem facing all evolving societies and it requires an ability to explain, foresee and transform. It can only be achieved by people who are both cultured and technically trained, that is to say, who are able effectively to carry out a specific task in the development process, in other words, have acquired technical competence in a specific field, but are also aware of the significance of their work in relation to the objectives and mechanisms of economic growth and the process of social change. For example, thorough knowledge of the mechanisms of agricultural development is required in varying degrees by the farmer and the agriculturist but they will not be able to appreciate the true significance of this process unless they see it in relation to the process of overall development, that is to say, in the light of the events and ideas which govern this development. The concept of general education must therefore be widened to include consideration of the objectives and the technical, economic and social components of socio-economic development. Rigid distinctions between the different 'subjects', petrified by traditional structures, should be weakened or destroyed. There is no justification for the distinction between technical and general education in a training which is based on development nor for the distinction between scientific and technical subjects: development is based on the dual ability to communicate and to act.

'Functional' training must always be based to some extent on multi-disciplinarity and teaching methods which involve team-work and thus prepare for inter-disciplinarity in action.

If men are to be helped to face the problems of evolving societies the cultural heritage of humanity must be used to explain the present by analysis of historical processes; but we must also learn to foresee the future. The teacher's repertoire is far better provided with models of the past than with plans for the future of society: we look backwards more often than we look ahead. But if we are to attempt to answer the questions of apprehensive young people and encourage the habit of looking ahead, it is at least as important to study the Meadows Report[19] or the Indicative World Plan for Agricultural Development.[20]

The desire to base our patterns of thought on the future will no doubt increase as we realise that development must be controlled and as young people insist that the educational system prepare them more effectively to face the life which lies ahead of them. The educational system should therefore teach pupils to draw up or analyse models of the future (long-term plans, development schemes, blueprints for society) enriched by the experience of past generations. If this is to be possible, a considerable effort will have to be made to renew present teaching equipment.

The process of creation-dissemination is the basis for economic growth and development. Technical progress requires inventors, extension workers and innovators and the progressive society is based on the transmission and dissemination of knowledge. But the way in which knowledge is disseminated is also important: in preference to straightforward instruction in tired and tested techniques 'under supervision', we favour 'community development methods' which would encourage the groups concerned to assume responsibility for the technical and social changes required. All should be aware of the importance of education, research and information and of their role in the process of development, and one of the main tasks of training in general should be to promote this awareness.

However, as we have seen, the creation-dissemination process is also a process of creative destruction and social change. When progress accelerates, the ability to change becomes a vital necessity. The acceleration of economic growth calls for greater occupational (and often geographic) mobility on the one hand and on the other soon makes knowledge acquired at school obsolete. The educational system must therefore meet this challenge in two ways: first, by preparing pupils for change by inculating a general awareness of the mechanisms of development and the mobility which they entail and secondly, by offering an opportunity for retraining and adjustment in life-long education.

It follows that teaching methods should develop the ability to 'learn to learn' by enabling pupils to acquire the technique of self-instruction and by facilitating access to and use of suitable educational institutions: 'open' laboratories, documentation centres and libraries, data banks, programmed learning, audio-visual aids, etc. 'The new educational ethos makes the individual the master and creator of his own cultural progress. Self-learning, especially assisted *self-learning, has irreplaceable value* in any educational system.'[21]

II. SPECIFIC FORMS OF RURAL AND AGRICULTURAL EDUCATION AND INTEGRATION PROBLEMS

1. *The transitional period*

The basic educational principles of universality, continuity, equality of opportunity, social relevance and orientation towards change and the problems of evolving societies are principles which affect all citizens. But they are seldom applied, and for this there are many reasons.

In almost all educational systems, agricultural training is a separate category: this is due to the low level of development in agriculture, the preservation of semi-archaic or traditional structures, preconceived views as to the capabilities of the rural population, the cultural heritage of the West, socio-political structures and lack of understanding of the requirements of evolving societies or of the tremendous effort which will have to be made in the next few years to supply our food and protect our biosystem. More often than not, agricultural education is a separate, closed system; rural youth have little or no chance of reaching certain levels of training; traditional teaching methods are used which have scant relevance to the socio-economic organisation of a developing agriculture; the processes of development do not figure on the syllabus; and the changes which take place in the agricultural sector are still, from time to time, explained by reference to exclusively agricultural types of analysis.

In certain cases, the specifically rural nature of the diplomas is looked upon as a means of ensuring that the pupil stays within the same social and geographical context: the educational system is used to prevent the flight of the rural population to the towns, i.e. to deal with a basically economic problem. The effectiveness of this segregationist approach can best be judged by results, which show that it accentuates feelings of frustration and inevitably leads to strife. The agricultural community recognises that educational segregation is based on, or will eventually produce, segregation in society.

Educational institutions which provide agricultural training are more often than not isolated and of a specific type; the children of the rural world who intend to remain faithful to their background are separated from those who take the 'royal road' of general education. If is often the Ministry of Agriculture and Rural Development rather than the Ministry of National Education that is responsible for education in the agricultural sector, an arrangement which is sometimes defended as allowing for better co-ordination between research, education and extension work in agriculture. However, experience shows that this alone will not ensure such co-ordination, nor is it in all probability necessary for it.

Agricultural education rarely forms a coherent whole when it is considered as a special category. Farmers, stock-raisers, foresters and specialists in land improvement or mechanisation are sometimes trained in separate establishments which are poorly co-ordinated, when it would appear obvious that there could be a common basic course for all those training for rural development work. It occasionally also happens that the different levels are poorly defined and that transfer from one step to the next is difficult if not impossible. The first world conference on agricultural education reached the conclusion that a great effort would have to be made to make agricultural systems of education more coherent.[22]

The rural world in its present form is the product of historical processes and is not adapted to the needs of evolving societies. Action must be taken as a matter of urgency to prevent part of mankind from suffering the consequences of economic policies and educational systems which look back rather than forward. It will however take time to integrate the rural world within the overall system of education and this for many reasons, the most important of which we feel to be the existence of a dialectical relationship between level of education and level of development. The training in critical analysis and the technical skills which can be obtained from the educational system contribute towards development; on the other hand, the number of educated personnel which can be absorbed by a given sector of activity depends on its degree of modernisation. However, this dilemma can be resolved by equipping sectors in the process of modernisation with organisations and services which will assist workers in the sector and by developing a system of life-long education which will be better equipped than any other to harmonise rates of progress in education and development.

We use the term 'transitional period' in connection with rural and agricultural education to designate the period of time necessary for rural education to be integrated within the overall educational system, and for the rural world to be made part of the content of overall education, starting from the moment when integration becomes a stated objective of the whole nation.

In this section we shall consider the different forms of rural education and agricultural training which exist at present and discuss integration problems while in the following section we shall consider the outlook for the future.

A. Basic training in the rural environment

1. Elementary education in the rural environment: the primary school

Sixty per cent of the world's inhabitants are members of farming families; many of them are illiterate. In the next few years, basic training for the farming community will rarely go beyond the elementary level. Although this training can be acquired in other ways, the primary school is particularly important in the rural world. Attempts made in the LDCs in recent years to provide elementary education for all by encouraging full attendance at school have ended in failure which can be explained both by conditions peculiar to the rural environment in these countries and by the unsuitability of the methods used.

Knowledge of certain features of the rural world is essential for *a proper understanding of training problems in the rural environment.*[23] The characteristics of the rural world are its material poverty — low family incomes, low level of public investment (lack of running water, electricity, etc.), poor local supplies (understocked shops) and so on — and its intellectual poverty — high rate of illiteracy, lack of newspapers and books, etc. The transistor radio is however quite common and is the main point of contact with the outside world.

Where primary schools exist, they very often lack the necessary intellectual and material equipment. Teachers follow a short course of general education and their vocational training is often neglected, though every now and again a particularly strong personality will be able to play an important part in local rural development or in encouraging young people to attend secondary schools. Attendance at primary schools is irregular and tends to fall off as the children grow older. The beginners' classes are overcrowded while classrooms for the older children are almost deserted: on average, 50 per cent of children leave primary school before completing the course. Many reasons are given, the most common being that the older ones are needed for work in the fields.

As a general rule, primary schools reflect the socio-economic environment and are judged on the results which this environment expects of them. It is generally recognised that primary schools are unlikely to bring about radical change in the environment; they alone will not enable the farmer to escape from his poverty. In such circumstances, the village-dweller sees the primary school as a way of escaping from poverty only to the extent that it will enable him to leave the land altogether. Young people also tend to see migration to the town as a way of escaping the hold of the social group, generally very strong in country areas.

Such being the net effect of a primary schooling in rural areas, some blame the education given and attempt to reform it. They call for a specific curriculum geared to the requirements of the rural world and for staff specially trained to teach such a curriculum. But this obviously runs counter to the expectations of parents who, in accordance with traditions inherited from the colonial period, see primary school as a means of escaping poverty by qualifying for jobs in the town.

The desire to 'ruralise' the primary school is characteristic of those who explain everything in terms of educational factors seen in isolation. In fact, as we have already said, the development of education and the modernisation of rural life go hand in hand. It is no doubt desirable that curricula should be adapted to the rural environment but this obviously cannot be the only method used to prevent the flight from the land. In any case, the 'ruralisation of the primary school' should not result in the opportunities open to the country-dweller being inferior to those of the town-dweller and encourage selection on the basis of social background rather than according to ability. The rural world in developed countries, in its struggle to achieve parity, is very conscious of the question of equality of opportunity: it realises that the structures of primary education, based as they are on nineteenth-century concepts, must be revised and calls for pre-school education, grouping of isolated primary schools, school transport, provision for educational guidance, etc.

If we are to analyse the role of the rural primary school in greater detail, we must state more clearly the functions which we expect it to fulfil.

2. *The functions of the rural primary school and what is needed to fulful them*

The rural primary school has four basic functions:

— to teach the basic skills of reading, writing and arithmetic;
— to inculcate attitudes and patterns of thought which correspond to the goal of rural and overall development;
— to be a genuine instrument of rural development; and
— to enable the more gifted pupils to go on to secondary school.

1. The primary school's first task is to teach the basic skills of communication (oral expression, reading and writing) and arithmetic. The high proportion of pupils who repeat grades or fail to complete their course would indicate that even these aims are ambitious. Failure can be ascribed to unsuitable teaching methods (too little incentive) but it is more the fault of the socio-economic environment itself (parents' attitudes, use of children for certain jobs on the land, etc.) and the irrelevance of school for those who expect to remain on the land (intellectually impoverished environment, lack of newspapers and books, reading considered a waste of time by adults, etc.).

There must be some incentive for attendance at school; it should not be seen as an obligation. For example, when subsistence farming gives way to market-orientated farming, the adult who, in order to sell his products, needs to read the weight on the scales, multiply this weight by a price per pound, etc. is strongly motivated to acquire the basic skills. This adult motivation may rub off on the child.

2. The primary school does not only impart basic skills; it also creates attitudes and patterns of thought which will affect the pupil for the rest of his life. As the main characteristic of agriculture is that it uses biological methods of production (plants and animals), the mental attitude to be encouraged is one of experimentation.

Change in the technological model of agriculture is based essentially on experimentation and demonstration. To prepare young people for technological change is to enable them to assess the effects of change. In such circumstances, the 'school garden' can be an instrument of general education and the true significance of manual work may become clear. In the same way, the organisation of small stock farms as part of the campaign to increase supplies of animal protein and of domestic science lessons designed to improve the balance of diet may not only help to raise living conditions in the surrounding district but be of real educational value.

Within the context of socio-economic development, the function of the primary school is to assist the child to establish a relationship with nature (observation and experimentation) and with other people and to make him willing to accept change. The primary school therefore plays a general role which involves more than the acquisition of basic skills.

3. The primary school can also play a part in rural development by picking out young people who show exceptional promise and making the school a meeting place where all the members of the rural community can pool their ideas.

It would no doubt be desirable for the primary school to encourage respect for the dignity of work on the land, to create a sense of vocation and to persuade gifted young country-dwellers to remain faithful to their background, and if the right methods are used this may be a practical possibility in certain circumstances. But, as we have said before, there is a danger of wishful thinking on this subject. No community can expect to keep its most gifted members if it does not offer them opportunities which match their abilities and their desire for change.

We have also indicated that the primary school could, by working together with extension services, encourage an experimental approach and a willingness to accept change. But here again one should beware of placing too much faith in the ability of the primary school to develop vocational skills, and in the usefulness of technical and vocational knowledge acquired at too early a stage, particularly in a traditional, conservative environment. The school can, however, help to achieve progress and change within a community, on certain conditions which we shall discuss at a later stage.

4. The various attempts at 'ruralisation', whose effectiveness is often questionable, should not make us forget that one of the functions of the rural primary school, as of all primary schools, is to detect the intelligence which the nation needs to carry out its development and encourage the most gifted, whatever their social background, to continue their education at secondary school. If the ruralisation of the primary school were to lead to *de facto* segregation, with access to secondary education and to the training of the nation's professional categories being reserved exclusively or preferentially to city-dwellers, we would have a situation that was humanly intolerable and should be denounced in the strongest possible terms.

Another problem is that of the criteria according to which the most able children are selected, that is to say, the problem of the content or prescribed syllabus for entry to secondary school. We should find out what place is given in this syllabus to biology and an experimental approach that requires a type of intelligence and form of training particulary useful for a child raised in the country.

If the 'ruralisation' of primary education excludes access to secondary education, we should not be surprised if farmers protest vigorously against it, realising that in the socio-economic context in which they live, education is their only chance of improving their children's position in society.

3. Other approaches to basic training

As a result of what may be termed the failure of primary schools to provide basic training for all, two new trends have developed in recent years: reform of the traditional type of primary school and a search for new approaches to the problem.

Certain countries are beginning to move away from the Western model which sees the primary school as the only answer and to make basic training a more integral part of the rural community. It is of course essential for these communities to take part in basic training; however, their success in organising education themselves will depend in the last analysis on the direction in which they are evolving and their ability to introduce new ideas. They will probably have this ability in the wake of a major social revolution in which the rural population has played a leading role or with which it was closely associated, in the context of cultural revolutions such as we have witnessed in China, or when power has been assumed by political parties which are resolved to base development on radical transformation of socio-economic conditions and of the educational system. However, in such circumstances, the social revolution leads to revolution in the school, not vice versa. Dynamic farming communities can help to organise a type of rural education which combines intellectual and manual work, adapting the time-sequence of training to the cyclical requirements of village life, mobilising all educational resources and giving significance to basic training within the context of a dynamic desire for change and renewal in the village itself. In such circumstances, the rural communities are likely to take measures to safeguard their children's rights and particularly their right to form part of the nation's professional categories by keeping open access to the necessary courses of training.

In the absence of exceptional circumstances which are particularly favourable to social and educational change, certain modifications can be introduced to ensure that basic training is more effective. For example, given the need for motivation, some feel that basic training should be provided at a later stage, say from 15 to 25 years of age rather than from 6 to 12 as is now the case. At this age, motivation to learn is stronger and there is more likelihood of young people being able to follow the new directions suggested to them.

The same arguments can be used to justify basic training for adults: in recent years, functional literacy training for adults has met with some success. Functional literacy work is a selective type of training in that it is offered only to those who are motivated to learn; and because adult motivation is usually connected with occupation, it is based on the learner's desire to do his work more efficiently. For example, when subsistence farming gives way to market-orientated agriculture, the farmer needs to read the scales, calculate his price, etc. If he is using new techniques, growing new crops, etc., it will be easier for him to read the pamphlets provided by the extension services than to memorise increasingly complex oral instructions. In this type of basic training, audio-visual aids, particularly radio and television (facilities permitting), can be extremely helpful, either with the support of community centres or used directly. Numerous experiments are being carried out in this field in many different countries.

B. Vocational training and life-long education

1. Vocational training in agriculture

This type of training, which is basically practical, can take several forms. It has been provided on an experimental basis immediately after completion of the primary course; it can almost be considered as life-long education when agricultural extension work is sufficiently concentrated and effective; it can also be provided in special educational institutions.

In some countries, pre-secondary school education consists of an elementary and an intermediate ('middle school') stage. The education given at the middle school focuses more on agricultural training and the teaching of crafts (a variety of rural crafts). Although this system makes it possible to postpone the stage at which vocational training starts, there is nevertheless a risk that it will still be applied too early, particularly if the children are not motivated and the environment itself is conservative. It also requires teachers who have received a good basic training and regularly attend refresher courses.

In Europe, quite satisfactory results were achieved by farming courses held immediately after completion of schooling and particularly those given by peripatetic agricultural instructions. These teachers, who had been specially trained, taught groups of young people in their late teens or early twenties at various focal points within a given area. Their effectiveness was due in a very large measure to their close collaboration with the extension services.

When agricultural extension services are sufficiently thick on the ground, they can provide information and training on a regular basis. They provide education in the true sense of the word if, in addition to handing on instructions or 'nostrums', they encourage the farmer to observe the changing conditions of production and assess the effect of technical changes for himself (functional training). By making farmers more eager to learn, they can play a decisive role in the further development of vocational training. They can make an important contribution to this process by organising courses varying in length from several days to several weeks on new techniques and types of production, etc.

Extension services can also make a very valuable contribution by picking out keen youngsters who are old enough to be able to exercise some influence on the traditional environment, willing to learn how to be successful farmers, and also if necessary successful promoters of rural development, and have the ability to do so. Such young people would be able to receive longer training in colleges specially established for the purpose.

Agricultural colleges, some of the objectives of which may be reminiscent of the 'farm schools' of nineteenth-century Europe, cannot hope to achieve satisfactory results unless they are thoroughly integrated in their socio-economic environment. This means that the production systems used must be judiciously chosen and suitable for use in the particular environment, bearing in mind the manpower available, the various technological possibilities, the nature of the infrastructure, etc. In such circumstances, 'farm schools' could play an important part in the dissemination of progress. They should work together with agricultural extension services and other services promoting rural development, and with the rural communities themselves. Their schedules must be geared to the rhythms of agricultural life. They should aim to provide the largest number of future farmers in the shortest possible time with an education based on the observation of facts and practical experience of production. The course should be of approximately the same length as the farm season and, where necessary, provide for a divison of time between the school and the family holding (sandwich course).

2. *Forms of further training for adults*

Economic growth as a process of creative destruction and development as a process of change call for a continuous process of reflection, training and information. Life-long education in a rural environment comprises the activities of the services responsible for information, extension work and community development in the agricultural, health and social fields, training courses in different subjects, the agricultural college which may take in established farmers as mature students, the various means of improving one's qualifications as individuals or in groups, training organised by youth movements, professional organisations, political parties, etc.

The aim of life-long education in a rural environment is not only to increase farmers' receptiveness and to assist in the dissemination of technical progress, but also to identify and train potential promoters of rural development. To the extent that these individuals are 'projected' by the community as a whole, they can play a key role both in the dissemination of progress and in the socio-economic organisation of the rural environment. They may help to remodel basic education, to extend the various forms of community action and to activate village life, in particular by encouraging women and young people to express their opinions. In the Western countries, rural youth played a leading part in exploring new ideas and forms of socio-economic organisation in agriculture. There is no doubt that young people in a position to express their opinions could make a major contribution towards the renewal of outmoded concepts and patterns of life in rural areas of the LDCs. Prospective young farmers will expect more and more to be able to do their work efficiently within a socio-economic context which enables them to develop as individuals. The refusal of the older general to understand these young people or their inability to provide an outlet for their aspirations could be a much more important element in their decision to migrate to the towns than the so-called irrelevance of the primary school to the rural environment.

3. The education of women

Although women have the same rights as men in the eyes of the law, this equality is not reflected in reality in the sphere of education: attendance rates are lower, while average length of training is shorter and access to certain schools and professions impossible even in advanced countries. Here the extension of mixed education is likely to lead towards real equality. In the LDCs, although the principle of equality is generally recognised, there are many adverse factors which have a cumulative effect and the education of women suffers as a result.

The IWP shows that living conditions in many farming households will for some time to come be dependent to a large extent on a subsistence economy. Modernisation of the subsistence economy is therefore essential if the material well-being of such families is to be improved.

The role of women can be decisive in improving food crops (for which they are responsible in many countries), in balancing the diet and improving the quality of meals, in hygiene and health, living conditions, local community affairs, village life, etc. As mothers and active participants in family and village life, women are in a position to have a decisive influence on trends in school attendance and rural development in general. The beneficial influence of women should be strengthened and extended by allowing women access to schools, by providing them with approximate extension services which place emphasis on health and household management in a rural environment and by allowing them to take more part in the deliberations of the councils and other bodies governing educational systems and rural life. Finally, women should be allowed broad access to agricultural extension services (household management in a rural environment) and to social services in general, where they could work for the good of the rural community.

4. Package projects

Application of the 'package project' principle to education means that education is made a 'component' of all development projects. socio-economic and educational measures are co-ordinated within the framework of a major project and 20 per cent, for example, of the total cost of the project is systematically set aside for training. It will readily be appreciated that the construction of a dam making it possible to irrigate land which until then was farmed dry calls for a carefully prepared programme of training and information including both experimentation and demonstration.

The advantage of the 'package project' is that it links training with changes taking place before the pupils' eyes; the desire to prepare themselves to cope with the effects of these changes upon their own lives should provide sufficient incentive. However, to be considered educational, such a project must not be content to deal with strictly technical aspects but should consider the significance and the scope of the project from the point of socio-economic development. This means dealing not only with the significance of the expected surplus and the advantages accruing to farmers but also with the distribution of the surplus within the community and its consequences for overall development.

Although the opportunity offered by a major project to implement an original training programme should not be rejected, it must be recognised that such projects are relatively rare and that basic training clearly requires a continuing type of motivation.

5. Community development

Community development proper occurs when the basic community unit assumes responsibility for its own development. This implies an organisation (collective decision-making), objectives and resources. These conditions are met to a greater or lesser degree in the basic collective units of socialist societies (collective farms, peoples' farms in Cuba, Chinese communes, etc.).

In market-economy countries, community development should be understood more as a series of measures co-ordinated at village level. Its aims are material (increased production and improved living conditions), educational (to transform traditional attitudes in the face of change) and social (to encourage a co-operative approach and various forms of joint action). The aim of community action can be summed up as 'helping farmers to help themselves'. It approaches this problem on a broad front and co-ordinates the activities of the different trained personnel involved in rural development: we feel that this in itself is very important. People with training in the fields of health, primary education, vocational training for farmers, adult education, household management in rural areas, agricultural extension work, social organisation, etc. should all be able to co-ordinate their activities at village level. In fact such co-ordination is often sadly lacking and the different services have been known to be at cross-purposes within the basic community unit. It would in such circumstances be very helpful if the community itself defined the assistance which it needed and itself assumed the role of co-ordinator.

But for a rural community to assume responsibility for its own development it must do more than define and co-ordinate assistance: it should be able to choose and implement modes of socio-economic organisation and define the content of community action. This may take several forms, from mutual assistance to the collective organisation of one or more 'basic community units', with the various types of co-operative action in between.

A dynamic community will plan its future, including that of its young people — though this will not necessarily depend solely on the future of the community. Some will have to agree to work as labourers in other sectors of activity if the community has not seen to it that they receive a training adapted to its needs. And however able the young people of the individual community, they will not be able to become leaders of regional or national development if the community does not insist that educational structures allow them access to secondary education or to other channels which lead to higher education.

C. Training for intermediate and senior agricultural personnel

1. Training for technical (intermediate) personnel

The integration of technical (intermediate-level) training for agriculture within an open, overall educational system, for example, in comprehensive schools which offer practical or more academic advanced courses of agriculture in the final year of both short and long courses of secondary education, is an objective which most countries, including developed countries, have not yet achieved. In recent years, however, the trend in developed countries has been to integrate technical training for agriculture more and more closely within the overall educational system, in regard to its structures (similar to those of general education), its curricula and methods (equivalent standards), its results (equivalent diplomas) and its links with the general educational system (bridge classes), which should in theory allow a maximum of choice and opportunity to change courses.

In most LDCs agricultural education continues to be a special category, often considered inferior, which leads young country-dwellers into what can only be called an educational ghetto. This approach to agricultural education produces *de facto* inequality in regard to access to education, a process which should ideally allow pupils to reach the highest level of which they are capable while at the same time respecting their essential freedom.

The segregation and the non-equivalence of diplomas which results from this approach are sometimes justified by reference to the special conditions in rural areas (schools which have experimental plots or model farms at their disposal) and to the need to keep trained agricultural personnel on the land. Although experimental plots are essential, very few of the 'model' farms attached to schools of agriculture are models which could be applied in the real conditions of production. In the long run, it is disastrous and in any case completely unacceptable to try to keep qualified technical staff in rural areas by refusing to grant equivalence of diplomas, access to higher education, etc.

Once again, this is not the way to halt the migration of qualified staff to the towns; this can only be done by modernising rural life and reorganising the system of promotion in the civil service in order to reward the 'field staff' whose role in the process of development is decisive, perhaps by means of a bonus for field work.

There are, however, other, more acceptable, arguments in favour of allowing agricultural education to remain a special category, in particular the view that the integration of technical agricultural education within the overall educational system must be achieved in stages. It would seem difficult in the short term to train intermediate-level personnel by altering general courses of education, as education is a slow process, particularly if provided in a language which is not that of the pupils. To make the training of such personnel part of general education would increase the length and cost of the course at a time when the LDCs need such personnel urgently and have limited resources at their disposal. The training of qualified agricultural personnel could, however, be improved in various ways during the transitional period. The following suggestions indicate possible lines of action:

1. Progressive integration of technical training for agriculture within the overall educational system by increasing the general educational content of the course and thus enabling the diplomas of agricultural education to be considered as equivalent to those of the corresponding stages of general education. This would involve, at the very least, the introduction of 'bridge classes' allowing for maximum choice and opportunity for changes of course;
2. The establishment of experimental general comprehensive schools with departments specialising in rural studies. The only way to minimise the stigma attaching to such departments is to modernise rural life, to ensure that all young people have a better understanding of the role of agriculture in the development process and to raise the status of intermediate-level agricultural development personnel;
3. Failing this, the establishment of agricultural comprehensive schools. The introduction at all levels of a 'common core' of classes compulsory for all pupils, whether they are going in for agriculture, animal husbandry, forestry, the manufacture of agricultural machinery, veterinary medicine, etc., is essential if the problem of agricultural development is to be considered as a whole. It would, *inter alia,* encourage a spirit of understanding and friendship between all those trained for agricultural development work and at the same time make it possible to reduce the number of institutions and teachers;
4. The organisation of full-time agricultural training courses in such a way as to allow for transfer from one stage to the next and in particular for access to higher education, if necessary by means of special classes;
5. Coherent organisation of the system of technical agricultural training, both as part of the school system and for adults.

As the Green Revolution continues, further training is particularly important for intermediate agricultural personnel, broadening their general education where necessary and enabling them ultimately to improve their position;

6. A comprehensive approach to the agricultural training system should make it possible to provide satisfactory and efficient structures for technical extension services. One of the major defects of these structures in many countries is the small number of intermediate-level personnel in relation to the number of graduates. Certain countries are aware of the disadvantages of this situation and are doing their best to remedy it;

7. The introduction, at all levels of education, of teaching designed to set agricultural development against the background of overall development. The basic purpose of such teaching, which comes basically under the heading of general culture, is to bring out the significance of the technical sphere of action;

8. The formation of teams of teachers which include full-time community development workers and call on the services of experts in the different technical fields (agriculture, animal husbandry, forestry). These teams should be familiar with plans laying down strategy and tactics for overall and agricultural development and with regional development plans or specific development projects being implemented in their area;

9. The introduction of teaching methods involving team work and pupil participation, particularly if the pupils are to be leaders of rural communities, professional organisations or multi-purpose rural co-operatives;

10. The formation of interdepartmental co-ordination committees (combining the Ministries of Education and Agriculture) to consider ways in which technical agricultural education could be made part of a functional overall educational system while at the same time catering for the specific needs of agriculture.

2. Training for senior (graduate) personnel

The training of senior (graduate-level) agricultural personnel, as seen in the light of the development process, raises many complex problems to which we cannot do justice here.[24] We shall therefore restrict ourselves to one or two general comments.

1. Higher agricultural education should be integrated in the overall educational system. This means that all the types of training offered by the system (and in particular technical agricultural education) should offer access to it, and that it should operate in relationship with other forms of higher education (integration with university studies) and be able to award all types of university degrees without exception (including the doctorate). Advanced agricultural studies should be based on a comprehensive view of higher education and not on narrow concepts which would make them a special category.

2. The need in the LDCs to adopt a comprehensive approach to rural development and to create a feeling of comradeship between all future promoters of this development, together with the limited supply of teachers and material equipment in these countries, makes 'agricultural centres' forming an integral part of a university preferable to specialised colleges. By the range of scientific disciplines they offer, the agricultural centres should train the different types of graduate needed by the nation: agronomists, veterinary scientists, rural economists, forestry experts, country planners, etc.

3. Like any other form of education, advanced studies in agriculture should be relevant to the nation's real needs, to development mechanisms and to plans for the future of society. This implies the adaptation of syllabus, levels of education and teaching methods to the nation's needs, not to mention preliminary revision of the grading system used in the civil service, which at present encourages excessively long periods of training which are not justified by present levels of development. Education should not try to give a training which will last a whole lifetime or to establish a definite hierarchy; it should make advanced full-time education part of a structure for life-long education.

4. Considerable attention should be devoted to life-long education and arrangements for enabling intermediate-level personnel to improve their qualifications and position. These two types of training are even more important in LDCs than in developed countries in view of the need for social justice, technolgical advance, shorter periods of full-time education, etc. The agricultural centres at universities should therefore regard the provision of such training as an essential part of their job.

Universities should show, in their willingness to change their structures, curricula and methods and in the importance they attach to agricultural education, that they are able to meet the needs of developing societies.

5. In Africa, in view of the expense of higher education and the small size and limited resources of several countries, international centres for agricultural education and further training of this type could be a practical and effective solution.

III. INTRODUCTION TO THE PROGRAMMING OF RURAL AND AGRICULTURAL EDUCATION

1. *Educational planning in evolving societies*

In Section II we examined the various forms of rural and agricultural education in their present context and the possibility of improving them during the transitional period. Our real objective is more ambitious, however, as we wish the rural population — farmers, intermediate agricultural personnel, etc. — to be fully educated individuals and the population of the nation as a whole to be aware of the importance and the role of the rural population in economic growth and the establishment of a new society. ' . . . any innovation in education admittedly runs into strong resistance, conscious and unconscious, practical and metaphysical. From the traditionalists, whom their opponents label outdated, and from speculators over the future, whom the former call utopian. From the inside, among educational structures, and from the outside, among politcal reactions.'[25]

We feel that this criticism and lack of understanding could be overcome to some extent if plans for education were defined with more reference to plans for economic growth, development and social progress. It is not our job to draw up plans for the future of society: the dynamics of society itself will look after that; what we must try to do is to understand and apply the dialectical relationship which exists between education and society. This approach takes us a long way from the quantitative planning practised in recent years. This type of planning is based on the forecasting of manpower requirements in the different sectors and it has its uses in certain situations. It provides figures which are essential when planning the allocation of funds, the rate at which educational establishments are built and where they should be sited, teacher-training programmes, etc.

These were major preoccupations in our earlier work[26] and in the appendix we describe some quantitative techniques which may prove useful. But the quantitative approach cannot take on its full significance unless it is integrated in a qualitative and institutional approach to planning. Moreover, we know that it is meaningless to plan the development of one economic sector in isolation from the others. In the same way 'it is no longer desirable to undertake educational reforms in piecemeal fashion, without a concept of the totality of the goals and modes of the educational process. To find out how to reshape its component parts, one must have a vision of the whole'.[27] In other words the planning of rural and agricultural education must be considered as part of the whole question of educational planning.

2. Qualitative planning

Many countries have begun to plan the development of their educational system in recent years. In 1963 Unesco founded an International Institute for Educational Planning[28] to be an international centre for advanced training and research. The Institute is also publishing a series of documents on the fundamentals of educational planning. At first planning was centred on economic forecasting, and in particular on the probable manpower requirements of the different sectors. The planning of agricultural education was therefore based on projections of the economically active agricultural population (Appendix, A). However, the planning of education is now focusing more and more on quality and institutions.

In June 1968, the OECD founded the Centre for Educational Research and Innovation (CERI), whose main objectives are to encourage and sustain the development of research in education, including pilot schemes, and to promote co-operation between the member countries in the sphere of research and innovation. The Centre has published many studies and works on educational innovation.

Models for the educational systems of the future belong in the main to one of the three following groups:[29]

(a) The future seen as a product of the past: the system is assumed to be static or periods of time are considered which are too short to allow for changes to be introduced or to have an effect;
(b) The future as an extrapolation of the present: the aim is to prolong and often to extend. The educational system becomes larger as higher qualifying standards are set and as population increases, but no fundamental changes are introduced in institutions or in methods. This is the quantitative approach, sometimes called 'first generation' educational planning (FGEP);
(c) The future seen in terms of a new society: the components of the future which relate to social and educational development are explored within the context of the dialectical relationship between education and society. This aspect of the future is determined by social dynamics and is very difficult to forecast: several different possibilities must be provided for.

On the basis of studies already published and of our foregoing analysis of the situation, we can make certain basic assumptions regarding future trends in education:

1. Efforts will be made to relate education to the problems of developing societies and in particular to those of the rising generations;
2. The traditional distinction between general education and vocational training will disappear and technical education will include a broad cultural component;
3. Life-long education will become more common and this will result in a decline in the importance of the school and of school diplomas and in the establishment of new educational institutions and centres to assist those who are educating themselves;
4. Teaching methods and the traditional role of the teacher will change as technological aids to education improve and social relationships evolve;
5. Increasing attention will be devoted during training to the acquisition of methods and to developing the aptitude to acquire technical skill in a given field. The type of education which produces 'walking encyclopaedias' should gradually give way to one which produces men who can adapt themselves to change or, better still, master it;

6. The pace and the content of education will tend to be better adapted to the individual, in accordance with the principle of life-long education and the diversification of institutions and methods. This trend may go hand in hand with the development of group teaching, the spirit and methods of which will instil an interdisciplinary approach in working life;

7. The invention and dissemination of new teaching methods in laboratories and documentation and demonstration centres specially created for the purpose will become an increasingly important aspect of the educational process. The 'traditional' phase of education, when each teacher prepared his own lessons, defining both content and method on an individual basis, should give way to a 'scientific' phase, characterised by division of labour (team teaching, use of advanced techology). Increased efficiency should not involve depersonalisation; in teaching as in other fields of activity, the scientific personality expresses itself through invention and innovation.

Figure 2 shows the creation-dissemination system at work in education. Although the processes of creation and dissemination are quite distinct, the system should be evaluated as a single whole.

A creative approach to education must be based on systematic organisation of methodological research, on original studies (case studies, educational games, blueprints of society, etc.) and on experimentation with or adaptation of new methods and instruments. Research into and experimentation with new methods are the 'R' and 'D' of the educational system. The dissemination of these methods may be based on pilot centres (demonstration) or on their immediate adoption by forward-looking educational institutions; in the latter case it would be essential to give such institutions a free hand and not to inhibit them with inflexible rules and regulations. Such institutions could belong to any one of the three sub-systems: they could be schools or universities or institutions providing basic training or life-long education for adults. In each of these sub-systems the institutions may be set up on public or semi-public initiative or the initiative may be provided by the 'users' themselves. Individual initiative could be particularly important in the field of adult education.

Educational institutions are a part of the 'learning society' in which training and information may be dispensed by many other bodies, including those belonging to the socio-cultural complex. Indeed, there is no reason why all social institutions should not form part of a democratic educational system that looks forward to the advent of a world in which human relationships have achieved a new refinement . . . a world with no pupils, no teachers and perhaps even no schools, where each is pupil and teacher in turn. This distant, perhaps idyllic picture has no place for the use of force, for social conflict or for the innumerable ways in which one man can impose his will upon others. Let us not forget that although the educational system is the product of a particular society, it can also help to bring a new

Figure 2. The creation-dissemination system in education

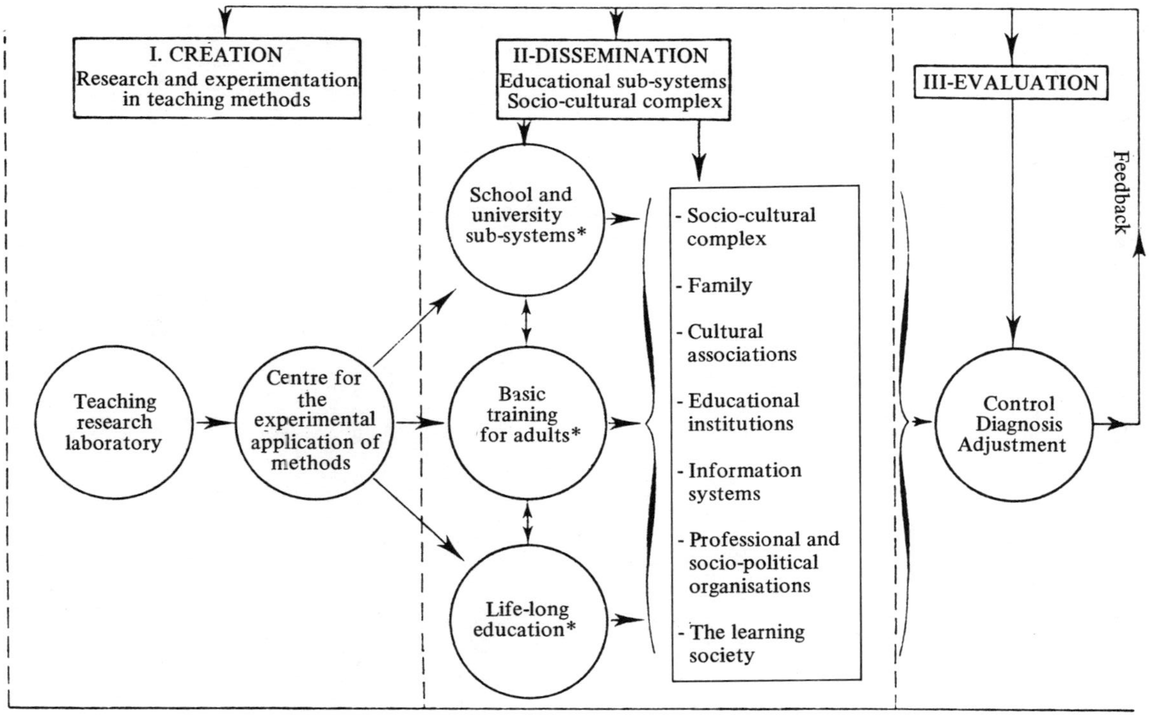

I. CREATION
Research and experimentation in teaching methods

- Teaching research laboratory
- Centre for the experimental application of methods

II-DISSEMINATION
Educational sub-systems
Socio-cultural complex

- School and university sub-systems*
- Basic training for adults*
- Life-long education*

- Socio-cultural complex
- Family
- Cultural associations
- Educational institutions
- Information systems
- Professional and socio-political organisations
- The learning society

III-EVALUATION

- Control
- Diagnosis
- Adjustment

Feedback

*Public or private educational institutions

society into being if it is free to invent, innovate and indulge in critical analysis of existing situations. Critical analysis and invention have a bearing on the educational system itself: it must therefore be judged as a whole, and 'feedback' mechanisms must be used to assist in the process of evaluation.

Assessment of the educational system's effectiveness as a creation-dissemination system may reveal a lack of research activity and a disinclination to invent or try out new methods, perhaps due to institutional or socio-political rigidity, and may be the point of departure for the introduction of new methods which are more in line with the objectives of developing societies.

3. Agricultural development and the development of education

Underdevelopment is not only a cultural phenomenon: it is also the product of a socio-political complex with low productive capacity and semi-archaic or traditional patterns of organisation. Education is a product of society. Education is also necessary for the development of a given society. It is the basis of the creation-dissemination system that triggers technical progress, which is the main component of economic growth and increased productivity of labour.

Development cannot be achieved without education but it cannot be achieved either without incentive, which could in many cases be provided by acceptable distribution of the economic advantages accruing from increased productivity.

Education is both the product of society and an instrument for bringing about change in society: it contributes towards economic growth by inventing new methods and promoting their use and, if it is allowed enough freedom, it can also contribute towards development by its critical analysis of existing situations. There is a dialectical relationship between education and society: social development and educational development are inseparable.

Our ultimate objective being the integration of agricultural education and agricultural development within the overall system of education and development, we shall now examine the outlook for the future, taking as our basis the relationship between education and society. In so doing, we shall consider the relationship between the successive stages of agricultural development and those of overall development and the relationship between education and the various forms of socio-economic organisation.

Whatever the form of socio-economic organisation, agricultural development always passes through three stages: based initially on subsistence farming, agriculture then becomes market-orientated and finally industrialised. Each of these stages can be paired with a corresponding phase of overall development, which moves from an agricultural economy through industrialisation to an industrial economy. As development and education are linked, each of these stages corresponds to clearly defined features of the educational system.

In certain rural areas of the LDCs, subsistence farming still dominates the agricultural scene and will continue to do so for some years to come. The main purpose of agricultural production is to provide food for the farmer and his family; society and economy are organised along traditional lines; production is determined in the main by biological processes; the productivity of labour is low and unreliable and money not widely used; farmers are poor and seldom able to purchase goods produced outside the agricultural sector. In such circumstances, the social group exerts strong pressure upon the individual and the village elders play an important role in the group; school is not expected to contribute towards the improvement of living conditions except in so far as it offers training for careers outside agriculture; as an instrument of social advancement, it operates mainly by enabling pupils to seek work in the towns.

But if schools, extension services and the various forms of adult education were to make it their aim to promote a more up-to-date approach to subsistence farming, they could effect a considerable improvement in living conditions in rural areas. Food crops and diet could be varied and made more nutritious; hygiene, health and housing conditions improved, and the school garden and demonstration plots of the extension services used to encourage an interest in experimentation and in new techniques and new types of crop suitable for use in the context of subsistence farming. The rural communities need help from outside at this stage and sometimes require the services of teachers who understand their problems and of professional community leaders who can advise them on a variety of subjects or if necessary put them in touch with the relevant administrative department. In such circumstances, the 'ruralisation' of education has its advantages, but it should not be allowed to bring with it segregation and discrimination which run counter to the insterests of the rural population.

It is inevitable that the educational system should reflect the preoccupations of a society which relies on subsistence farming for its existence. It should, however, be able to find many ways of improving living conditions during this stage, in the sphere of nutrition, health, housing – in fact all the major objectives of human activity.

The educational system can also help to prepare for the next stage of agricultural and social development. Schools can spot gifted children who should, given the necessary training, be able to play a useful part in the process of rural and overall development. Extension services and adult education can introduce commercial crops as well as encouraging a more enlightened approach to subsistence farming proper; they too can pick out individuals who have a responsible approach to rural development and to the long and arduous struggle to change the social structures of rural communities. Thanks to the active assistance of the educational system, and within the overall context of national development, agriculture will gradually become more market-orientated as the agricultural population dwindles and as the urban population grows and its *per capita* food requirements increase.

For many people, the modernisation of agriculture means the transition from subsistence farming to the market-orientated stage. But one should beware of supporters of modernisation who do not base their calculations on models of evolving societies: as we have seen, the importance of subsistence farming will continue to increase in some areas and, wherever an attempt is made to introduce market-orientated agriculture, the modernisation of subsistence farming will be a necessary preliminary before agricultural goods can be produced for sale outside the sector. The question of subsistence agriculture should not therefore be neglected, as is all too often the case.

During the 'market-orientated' stage, an increasing proportion of agricultural production is sold outside the sector. As subsistence agriculture gives way to market-orientated agriculture, major transformations will be taking place in society as a whole (extension of industry and services, urbanisation, etc.) as well as in the agricultural sector itself (new forms of socio-economic organisation, new production systems, improved productivity of labour, etc.). Money will come into use in the agricultural economy, trade will increase, an effort will be made to organise transport and markets and professional organisations, co-operatives and credit institutions will gradually come into being. At this stage of development, as the agricultural community becomes more outward-looking, there may well be an upsurge of interest in primary education and functional literacy. The changes taking place before their eyes will provide the necessary incentive for both young and old. The primary school will be able to encourage an experimental attitude to nature and help develop a spirit of team-work. Vocational training for farmers and a dense network of extension workers backed up by applied research and experimentation in the field will become a vital necessity. Farm management, marketing, credit arrangements and the development of co-operatives are all subjects which should be given greater prominence in curricula at this stage.

Once rural development gets under way there will be a place for farmers in whom a pioneering approach has been instilled by a vigorous further training campaign, for militants and youth movements, as well as for the active participation of women, of extension workers both with specialised and more general skills, of experts on planning, land reform, agricultural markets, credit, co-operative techniques, food industries, etc.

The most developed countries have now reached the stage where agriculture, from being market-orientated, becomes industrialised. Intensive use is made of technology and the productivity of labour is very high. The word 'peasant' with its rather derogatory overtones can no longer be used. The agricultural sector is composed of farmers who fulfil a specific economic function in a society into which they are fully integrated and have achieved a mature understanding of the development process and all its implications.

4. Agricultural development and the overall educational system

The ease with which rural education can be integrated within the overall educational system and the justification for its integration will vary from one stage of rural and national development to another. We do feel however, bearing in mind present conditions in the LDCs and the requirements which their future development makes of them, that integration is to be preferred to segregation.

The integration of rural education within the national system as a whole can be justified on grounds of effectiveness, justice and a particular concept of society. Arguments based on effectiveness relate both to agricultural development and to the development of the nation as a whole. As we have seen, humanity will not be able to cope with the unprecedented increase in world food requirements unless the conditions of agricultural production are radically transformed and this in turn will not be possible unless corresponding changes take place in socio-economic structures and unless rural education itself is given a new lease of life.

Agriculture should endeavour to attract dynamic young men rather than repelling them, as it often does at present. It must offer such men the opportunity to improve their occupational skills in up-to-date working conditions without imprisoning them in an educational ghetto which prevents them from fulfilling their personal aspirations. Talented, dynamic young men who are aware of the choices available to them will never willingly embrace a career which offers no prospects and which closes certain doors to them, whether in education or in other spheres. Agriculture could secure the services of such men at each stage of its development by creating dynamic rural development networks. This nearly always means battling against the dead-weight of bureaucracy and encouraging men with a truly creative and original approach to problems. It also means rewarding people for the contribution which they actually make to development rather than for the examinations which they have at some time managed to pass. This could perhaps be done by means of special allowances for those who work 'in the field' or by bonuses for good results.

The integration of the rural world within the national educational system can also be shown to be an effective means of promoting overall development. To achieve maximum effectiveness, development must mobilise all the nation's human resources, leaving no source of talent untapped. Each individual, whatever his social background, must be enabled to achieve the maximum of which he is capable in the subjects for which he is most suited, and this will only be possible if the system of basic education, guidance, restreaming (change of course) and selection is open to all.

The principle of integration can also be upheld on grounds of social justice, and in particular by reference to the concept of educational democracy, on which equality of opportunity is based. It can, finally, be justified by the desire to create a united nation. No one can hope to achieve this aim through an educational system in which farming and country areas are treated differently from others. If the rural population is not to form a category apart in the nation as a whole, it should not form a category apart in education either. Rural and agricultural education should therefore be an integral part of the national educational system. In fact, when we say integration, we also imply that all citizens must be made aware of the role played by agriculture in the nation's development and of the ways in which the countryside can be integrated into the life of the society as a whole. It is in fact the whole educational system which must be 'ruralised'.

This does not mean that curricula and methods must be identical throughout the educational system, but rather that there should be a common core and arrangements enabling pupils to choose their course and move freely from one to another, using 'bridge classes' as links, etc. An integrated system which nevertheless met the practical requirements of society could include a 'top class' in the final year of each stage of the educational process which prepared pupils for a specific job or role in society. The same end could equally well be achieved by a system of life-long education which offered individuals training, refresher or re-training courses at any stage in their lives, irrespective of previous school career and academic qualifications.

Institutional planning should pave the way for training for those engaged in agricultural development work to be progressively integrated with overall development by setting up *ad hoc* committees to examine the implications of the process.

5. Agricultural development and specialised training

We have already established the need for the LDCs to intensify their efforts to achieve agricultural development if the threat of famine and a halt to overall development are to be averted. The training of those who will be called upon to take part in the process must be geared towards the integration of agricultural development within the context of overall development. In varying degrees, it will give them all a basic grounding in the physical, biological and human sciences as they affect the life and work of rural and farming communities and will teach them an experimental approach and techniques which will enable them to promote development, taking into account the resources and forms of socio-economic organisation which exist at present or which can be expected to exist in the future. Their training should accordingly include three basic components:

1. Analysis of the mechanisms of socio-economic development (general training);
2. Acquisition of scientific principles and an experimental approach to problems, in which biology will play an important part (scientific education); and
3. Training in the techniques of socio-economic transformation.

This will integrate general with vocational education, the use of specific techniques with scientific principles and the study of social realities with the study of ways of bringing about change. Here we define general education as the training which all citizens should receive to be able to understand and evaluate historical patterns of development, the present-day world and the main features of the future towards which society seems to be moving. As such it should obviously form part of the common core. Basic training in science could also be part of the common core, taking the form of courses based on biology which would prepare pupils for more specialised courses in agriculture, veterinary science, medicine, etc. Training in the use of techniques would demonstrate the way in which scientific principles can be applied to agriculture. Highly specific or functional instruction would be linked with more theoretical general and scientific subjects.

The total field to be covered is thus immense: it may be necessary in some cases to limit it ('short course') or in others to extend it by further specialised studies ('long course'). In any case, it is clearly always possible to combine specific instruction with the common core. Such training, which incidentally calls for a certain interdisciplinarity in approach, should produce people with both technical qualifications and general education. It is a deliberate departure from the purely scientific course which, although it can be a useful preparation for teaching or research work, is not suited to the needs of those who must operate within the context of socio-economic realities.

Training for agricultural development can be acquired in many ways: at school or university, as basic training for adults or as part of life-long education. The relative importance of these different channels will depend on the historical and geographical context and on the stage of development reached.

In the LDCs adult education is necessary in order both to remedy the high level of illiteracy, which is a legacy of the past, and to ensure the future success of agricultural progress based on the use of technology. What is therefore needed is a plan to co-ordinate the different sub-systems which contribute towards the training of those engaged in agricultural development work.

6. *Agricultural development and teaching methods*

The teaching methods used in training for agricultural development will be based on the principles governing teaching methods in general but will be adapted in various ways to the subject matter concerned.

As the two essential components of the process of agricultural production are man and his natural environment, the acquisition of methods of analysis relating to this context and the inculcation of a willingness to experiment are particularly important. Such things cannot be learnt from books, but only from observing, checking and interpreting the results of practical experiments. Moreover, as the ultimate objective is to train men who will be able to play their part in enabling agriculture to move as rapidly as possible from a semi-archaic or traditional stage to a more progressive one, the acquisition of techniques must be supplemented by an ability to decide in the light of existing socio-economic structures on the time and procedure best suited for the introduction of these new techniques. What is needed in most cases is a less bookish approach to agricultural training and greater emphasis on practical experience and the requirements of development.

Teaching methods used in agricultural education should be a training for change on the basis of consideration of development models. This is why the Indicative World Plan for Agricultural Development is in our view an educational document of the utmost importance, showing clearly that as the world's population grows and surface area per inhabitant shrinks, agriculture in most world regions will have to be intensified. It suggests different ways of bringing about this intensification and specific 'subjects' which would be taught — for example, the production and use of proteins, water resources management and use, ways of increasing production capacity, the preservation of natural resources, etc.

Little research has been carried out into methods of training for agricultural development; they are in the main traditional in approach, based on Western, individualist models which emphasise the pupil-teacher relationship, this despite the fact that types of education which place emphasis on individual achievement are seldom a good preparation for the close social relationships characteristic of rural life. Mutual assistance is an important feature of traditional forms of production, and community development tends to reinforce group solidarity inasmuch as it encourages the group to produce its own leaders; in such circumstances, agricultural and other co-operatives are generally felt to be destined to play an important role. In most cases it will therefore be desirable to have teaching methods which instil the habit of team-work.

Teaching pupils to learn means teaching them ways in which they can acquire knowledge on their own, teaching them methods of thinking and reading, teaching them how to use bibliographical data, filing systems, audio-visual equipment, etc. as well as making them more eager to extend their knowledge and take advantage of the opportunities offered by life-long education. In short, the teacher's task is to create the conditions necessary for a process of assisted self-learning.

Life-long education, which combines periods of intensive training with periods of assisted self-learning, calls for revision of present concepts of the role of educational institutions in society. The barriers between these institutions and the rest of society will be gradually removed — for example, their libraries will be open not only to their own pupils and students but if possible to all members of society; courses offered will be given a wide circulation to all those interested in them in the form of video-cassettes, etc. Life-long education may also require the establishment of special documentation centres which should be able to make teaching material and aids available to any organisation which requests them.

Life-long education implies a new approach to the use of mass media, in particular television, as these are exceptionally important for isolated rural settlements. However, the experimental promotion of television in rural areas (in many countries) has shown that it is not easy to find a really effective way of using these media. Provision must be made for feedback of consumer reactions, accompanying documentation to permit deeper consideration of the subject matter, programmes involving the use of two or more different media, evaluation of results, etc.

Teaching methods should change as more technological aids to teaching are introduced: in the most up-to-date schools of agriculture, computers are already being used to aid decision-making games by simulating the management of farms and other enterprises concerned with agriculture and food production, to construct models for the future evolution of society, for development planning, etc. There is still a long way to go before audio-visual methods are fully integrated into teaching practice but it can already be predicted that the combination of audio-visual methods and computers will be increasingly important for those who are teaching themselves or who live some distance from their teacher.

These trends are bound to have an effect on the training of educators involved in rural development. By educators we mean not only teachers in the traditional sense of the term but also those in charge of life-long education organisations or classes, the staff of self-learning centres, agricultural extension workers, etc. In addition to the agricultural training which all involved in agricultural development require to a greater or lesser degree, special attention should be paid to training in instructional methods and techniques and a more detailed analysis of development mechanisms.

7. Concluding considerations

The basis for industrialisation and for the development of individual and collective services is an increase in the productivity of agricultural labour. In fact, the single task of feeding humanity will be one of such Herculean dimensions in the coming years that the view that the world's farmers need only guidance and supervision, not education, is not only false but dangerous and should be vigorously opposed. If we are to avoid famine and make the best use of our natural resources at the same time as ensuring their preservation for future generations, we must mobilise humanity's intelligence and not simply its energy. Unfortunately, the present educational systems of the LDCs, which are a legacy of the past and the product of a variety of different influences, largely fail to meet the needs of evolving societies.

As we see it, not only agricultural and rural education but the whole educational system should be 'ruralised'. All citizens should be aware of the problems of national development and the role of agriculture in this process. They should also know how the productivity of labour can be increased, for this is a prerequisite for the construction of a new economy and with it of a new society. National unity will never be achieved by educational segregation; men will not be kept within a limited geographical area or sphere of activity for long by the device of the educational ghetto.

The chains of the rural world are something there is no getting away from, and in the less developed countries, the rural population will actually increase in absolute numbers during the coming years. The educational system must recognise this fact and aim to meet the challenge it presents by adapting the education provided to a specific environment, without at the same time causing educational segregation which would rightly be interpreted as social segregation.

Agriculture will not attract talent unless it offers the prospect of self-fulfilment on the professional and personal planes. The former is usually out of the question without sweeping changes in the technical, economic and sociological conditions of agricultural production; and it so happens that the needs of mankind as a whole are now such as to make the modernisation of agriculture a world-wide necessity.

Personal self-fulfilment requires that an individual be able at all times to express himself and his ability to the full without suffering restrictions imposed on the basis of his social background, race or, worse still, the course which for one reason or another he was obliged to follow at school in his youth.

The desire for economic effectiveness, social justice and a more humane society should make life-long education the corner-stone of the educational system. The school, a product of Western civilisation which has become so bound up with the socio-economic system that it is not only the sole purveyor of officially recognised knowledge but often determines job and salary too, should gradually be done away with. Societies with their eyes turned to the future have no place for such anachronisms, which should progressively disappear as life-long education for all is introduced, with periods of training alternating with periods of work and a variety of different courses and opportunities offered to all, in short with the advent of the 'learning society' described in the report of the International Commission on the Development of Education. But this process will require much patient effort and, unless society as a whole supports it, our changes of success are small indeed.

We have learnt from experience that the university graduate is no more eager for change than the members of other social groups; in fact, his scientific view of the world may lead him to the conclusion that the educational system itself has a scientific basis. Educational reformers know that the strongest opposition will be met from the many supporters of titles and privileges and of the social order associated with them.

The real significance of educational reform is to be seen in the context of the dialectical relationship between education and society; we feel that once a society becomes aware of its evolving needs and determines to take action to supply them, the major obstacle in the way of educational reform has been overcome.

8. The role of international co-operation

International co-operation is basically the sharing of all the world's experience: it should throw light on the decisive role of historical and geographical contexts and at the same time distinguish the universal principles underlying educational systems from the features associated with a particular context or environment. It should also encourage experimentation with new methods and approaches and facilitate the transfer of innovatory educational methods and technical aids. This was what the International Commission on the Development of Education had in mind when it proposed the establishment of an International Programme for Educational Innovations.[30]

As we have shown, the education of farmers, other categories engaged in agricultural development and the rural population in general calls for urgent action and all the imagination, inventiveness and determination which can be mustered to deal with a problem of such vast proportions. Three international organisations, FAO, Unesco and ILO, have shown great concern in regard to the problem of agricultural training and information. They have set up a Joint Advisory Committee on Agricultural Education, Science and Training, as evidence of their desire to co-ordinate their activities in this sphere, and in 1970 organised the First World Conference on Agricultural Education. This conference, held in Copenhagen, made it possible to obtain a comprehensive picture of the present situation and future prospects in this field.[31] The Joint Advisory Committee is to promote the exchange of new ideas and experience in regard to educational methods, organisation and technology, and will encourage the integration of rural and agricultural training into national education systems.

In this sphere, as in others, it is very important to set the future of the rural and agricultural world against the background of the development of society as a whole. For all these reasons, we feel it to be particularly important that the International Programme for Educational Innovations should devote special attention to the problems of education in agriculture and the rural world in general. In this sphere, as in the educational system as a whole, there should be more experimentation centres whose suggestions should be evaluated in accordance with pre-arranged procedures. Education alone will not guarantee agricultural development, but there can be no doubt that education is an essential ingredient of the development process. The many works published by international organisations or written with their encouragement and the principles which they have drawn up in recent years make them particularly well suited in our view to contribute towards a clearer awareness of the relationship between education and development and towards the introduction of educational systems which are more relevant to the goals of evolving societies. The fact remains that the renewal of educational systems proceeds in the last analysis from the socio-political philosophy peculiar to each nation and the social forces actuating it.

APPENDIX: TECHNICAL NOTE ON THE QUANTITATIVE PLANNING OF VOCATIONAL TRAINING IN AGRICULTURE

This note sets out only to suggest some techniques which can be used in quantitative planning for a clearly defined educational system. As we have seen, the definition of the system itself will be determined by qualitative and institutional planning. We shall consider in succession methods of projecting the working agricultural population (A), of determining the training targets to be reached (B), of estimating output and 'enrolment' (C) and of calculating costs and investments (D). In each case, we shall base our calculations on a hypothetical zone (Z).

I. PROJECTION OF THE WORKING AGRICULTURAL POPULATION

The simplest approach is to base educational planning on projections of the employment situation. However, as training to intermediate or upper intermediate level may last from five to ten years, care must be taken to ensure that the period covered by the plan is long enough for the educational system to be adjusted to the objectives set.

Changes in the size of the agricultural population are determined by birth rate and by the net rate of migration from agriculture, which in turn is determined by increased activity in non-agricultural sectors and the resulting demand for transfer of agricultural manpower. The agricultural population is to some extent a pool of manpower on which other sectors draw according to their needs. In such circumstances, the agricultural population can be described as residual. The development plan provides for distribution of the working population between the sectors on the basis of population growth and the expansion of activity in each sector.

A fairly clear picture of demographic trends in agriculture can be obtained by the following method: P_a, P_i and P represent the agricultural population, the industrial population and total population respectively and rp_a, rp_i and rp the corresponding growth rates.

If
$$\frac{P_a}{P} = \alpha_a \qquad \frac{P_i}{P} = \alpha_i$$

the increase in total employment can be expressed as:

$$rp = \alpha_a \ rp_a + \alpha_i \ rp_i$$

which gives:

$$rp_a = \frac{rp - \alpha_i \ rp_i}{\alpha_a}$$

Let us assume that the increase in total population is equal to the increase in the birth rate — of the order of 2.5 per cent per annum, for example — and that:

$$\alpha_a = 0.7 \qquad \alpha_i = 0.3 \qquad r_{P_i} = 5\%$$

The result will be:

$$r_{P_a} = \frac{2.5 - 5 \times 0.3}{0.7} = 1.4\%$$

This situation is typical of the LDCs: the weighted growth of the non-agricultural population is lower than the increase in the birth rate (although this sector of the population has a high rate of growth, it forms only a small proportion of the total population) and the agricultural population continues to increase in absolute value. This increase in absolute value is sometimes accompanied by migration from agriculture which gives a rate of 2.5 − 1.5 = 1%. This migration represents a section of the population which will need training for non-agricultural activities.

The corresponding model for developed countries would be:

$$r_P = 1\% \quad \alpha_a = 0.1 \quad \alpha_i = 0.9 \quad r_{N_i} = 1.5$$

which gives:
$$r_{P_a} = \frac{1 - 0.9 \times 1.5}{0.1} = -3\%$$

If the present size of the agricultural population and its rate of growth are known, its size at the end of the planning period can be estimated. Let us assume that the population at that time in Area Z will be 5 million.

When agriculture is based on the family unit, it is advisable to have calculations rather on the number of families. If the average family has five members there will be approximately one million families in the area. However, the number of families does not necessarily correspond to the number of holdings. If farming is organised on a capitalist or collective basis, the number of holdings would obviously be much smaller than the number of families. Even in areas where farming is based on the family unit, there may be some families who have no land of their own and work for wages, either outside agriculture or on a holding worked by several families. Projection of employment trends should therefore include projection of the number of holdings, bearing in mind developments taking place in this field.

II. DETERMINATION OF TRAINING TARGETS

We shall consider first the training of those working in agriculture and then that of the personnel staffing agricultural and para-agricultural organisations and services.

A. Vocational training for those working in agriculture

1. Determination of the number to be trained annually

The working agricultural population of area Z, in which agricultural structures are based on the family unit, consists mainly of heads of holdings and the male or female members of their family who help them. Our calculations will be based on the estimated size of this population at the end of the period covered by the plan.

Assuming an average working life of forty years (15 to 55), the average annual rate of replacement at the end of the plan will be:

$$\frac{5,000,000}{40} = 125,000$$

which therefore represents the number who have to be trained annually.

Let us assume in the first place that priority is to be given to the training of future heads of holdings. The rate of replacement of heads of holdings will be more rapid than that of the working population as a whole as they have a shorter period of activity: they will not assume responsibility for the holding until the age of thirty, for example, at the earliest. If the average period of activity of the head of holding is thirty years, the number of young people who will have to be trained annually as heads of holdings will be:

$$\frac{1,000,000}{30} = 33,000$$

The proportion of the working population which receives training and the methods of training used will depend on the educational system, on present percentages of trained manpower, on the planned rate of development, etc.

2. The structure of training

If, for example, it were decided to give 10 per cent of the annual number to be trained as future heads of holdings full-time training (as given in vocational training centres), this would mean an annual intake of 3,300.

It can safely be assumed that most future heads of holdings would be men. If it was felt that their wives should have received equivalent training the annual intake would be 6,600. In this case 4.5 per cent

$$\left[\frac{6,600}{125,000}\right]$$

of new entrants to the working population in the area would have received full-time training.

If the working agricultural population had, for practical purposes, previously received no vocational training, the proportion of trained people in the agricultural population as a whole at the end of the first course of training would be:

$$\frac{6{,}600}{5{,}000{,}000} = 0.13\%$$

This is a very small proportion and shows clearly the need for adult training programmes to be introduced simultaneously with full-time schooling, a course of action also justified by the need to accelerate agricultural development in the short term and train men who will immediately be able to assume some responsibility for development.

If in order to have an adequate 'leaven' for rural development purposes the aim were to provide vocational training for 10 per cent of all heads of holdings (male and female), i.e. a total of 200,000 by the end of ten years, training would have to be organised as follows:

full-time training	10 × 6,600	=	66,000
adult education			134,000
	Total		200,000

The output of the adult education system would thus be doube that of full-time training.

This rough outline is intended to underline the importance of adult education, if, as is often the case in the LDCs, little or no vocational training has previously been offered to farmers. Even so, we have only allowed for the training of 10 per cent of heads of holdings; a considerable effort would therefore need to be made if the remaining 90 per cent – not to mention all those members of their families who help them – were to be trained as well. This could perhaps best be done by providing short training courses for adults, whose organisation would depend on the rate of development and the techniques to be taught. Extension networks providing instruction in techniques appropriate to the differing stages and the varying pace of development would also have to be established, together with other related services.

B. Training of extension workers and community development organisers

The number of extension workers to be trained will depend on growth objectives and on present levels of training and information in the farming community. The number of farming families per extension worker will depend on a variety of factors. The experts of the IWP are of the view that in the LDCs 'a general objective of one full-time field-level extension worker per 1,000 farm families is a practical one giving reasonable coverage and within most countries' resources'.[1] This 'reference norm' will have to be adjusted to the particular requirements of each area. Application of this norm to our area Z which contains approximately one million farms gives a figure of 1,000 extension workers.

'Field-level' extension workers can be trained by a short (lower intermediate level) or long (intermediate level) course of secondary education, by various types of adult education for farmers and other people with suitable qualifications or experience who wish to change their occupation and by courses specially designed to enable, for instance, technical staff at lower intermediate level to move up to intermediate level.

The effective operation of extension services requires a reasonable ratio of senior (short or long courses) to intermediate staff. The IWP experts feel that a ratio of 1 to 5 would be satisfactory.[2] This means that 200 senior staff would be required to fill administrative posts and supervise work in the field in area Z.

When farming is based on the family unit, most supporting services will be external to the farm. They will be provided either by the State or by professional organisations.

The public authorities will need intermediate and senior administrative personnel, apart from those employed in the extension services, to staff government departments and area offices responsible for land reform, plant and animal protection, conservation, statistics, market organisation, etc.

The size and organisation of these services may vary considerably from one country and from one phase to another. (FAO proposes from 20 to 60 per cent of the manpower required for the extension services.)

As agriculture becomes more market-orientated, the importance of the private sector increases. Agricultural and food industries, distributors of agricultural equipment and products, farm cooperatives, credit institutions, etc. will be able to employ increasing numbers of intermediate-level agricultural staff. As a rule of thumb, we can say that the number of middle-level grades required in related services and professional organisations will be approximately half that required in the extension services. In area Z, we shall therefore need 1,500 intermediate staff and 200 senior grades.

Staff will also be required for teaching and research work. Calculation of these requirements will be more complicated: factors which must be borne in mind are the type of training given, the organisation and number of training centres, teacher-pupil ratios, etc. Different assumptions could be made and results compared.

Before estimating the number of teachers required to train intermediate-level personnel, it is necessary to estimate the number of such personnel who will be needed.

III. DETERMINATION OF EXPECTED 'OUTPUT' AND PUPIL NUMBERS

The average annual output will depend on the targets to be reached, the numbers currently available and the time allowed for achievement of the targets. In area Z for example, the estimated numbers of intermediate and upper intermediate personnel needed for direct assistance to rural development are 1,500 and 300 respectively. If 500 intermediate-level personnel are already available, the plan will provide for the training of a further 1,000.

An allowance must however be made for replacement of existing personnel (at a rate of approximately 3 per cent per annum) and net migration abroad or to other activities. People trained in agriculture tend to seek new outlets if their working and living conditions, relative salary scales, etc. are not satisfactory.

Trends in technical cooperation are likely to have a considerable effect on the number of personnel to be trained. The trend at present is for foreign (expatriate) personnel to be replaced by nationals. Lastly, allowance must be made for the migration of nationals who have received agricultural training to other countries, which in some LDCs occurs on quite a considerable scale.

Let us assume that in area Z the total number of intermediate-level personnel to be trained is 1,200. Annual output will be determined on the basis of length of course. As intermediate-level personnel require three to six years full-time training, it would be safe to take ten years as the average length of all types of training (though this will depend on foreseeable output in the light of the numbers at present undergoing training). Thus in area Z annual output should be 120. Student numbers will depend on the type of course (full-time or otherwise), on the length of course, etc. But some allowance will need to be made for transfers (intermediate-level personnel trained for work in agriculture who take jobs in other sectors), drop-outs (students who leave before completing their course) and grade repetition. When all these are taken into consideration, much higher student numbers are called for. This is demonstrated in the calculations set out below, in which the percentages have been chosen arbitrarily, they draw the reader's attention to the need to make allowance for these factors when determining the number of students required.

In all, an additional enrolment of 60 per cent must be allowed for transfers, drop-outs and grade repetition and the ratio of students starting the course to those who finally qualify will be $\frac{176}{100} = 1.76$, a figure which is not surprising when all things are considered. Indeed it might well be higher, as we have made the rather unlikely assumption that all students who take the final examination will pass it. A further allowance should therefore be made for failure rate at this stage.

Table 6. Determination of additional enrolment to be allowed for a three-year full-time course of training

Class	Calculation of number	Number	
Final year	(a) Number of qualified intermediate-level staff required	100	
	(b) Allowance for transfers (25%)	25	
	(c) Number to qualify	125	
	(d) Allowance for drop-outs (10%)	13	
	(e) Allowance for grade repetition (5%)	7	
	Number of students in final year (c + d + e)		145
Second year	(a) Number of students to move up from second year (145−7) =	138	
	(b) Allowance for drop-outs (10%)	14	
	(c) Allowance for grade repetition (5%)	7	
	Number of second-year students		159
First year	(a) Number of students to move up from first year (159−7)	152	
	(b) Allowance for drop-outs (10%)	16	
	(c) Allowance for grade repetition (5%)	8	
	Number of first-year students		176
	Total number of students		480

These calculations give some indication of the high cost of full-time training, due partly to the students' poor motivation (drop-out rates) and lack of ability (grade repetition and exam failures) and partly to the quality of the educational system itself. Motivated adults with experience of rural life could probably be trained with less expense and more satisfactory results.

The number of teaching staff required should be based on the number of students. For upper secondary education, the pupil/teacher ratio should be of the order of fifteen to twenty pupils to one teacher, if allowance is made for technical and laboratory assistants, field-work instructors, etc. The recruitment and training of teachers should be planned over the long term as a long period of training will be necessary.

IV. CALCULATION OF COSTS AND CAPITAL REQUIREMENTS

The estimates given above and the ratios used are only intended to be a rough guide, but they probably correspond fairly closely to realities. However, they cannot be expected to be universally valid or to be applied to every situation. Once targets, methods, student and staff numbers, etc., have been fixed, building and equipment requirements have to be assessed, costs calculated and the amount of capital needed estimated. The cost of agricultural training over an appropriate period can then be compared with the cost of other agricultural development projects, relating to rural infrastructure and facilities (roads, water and power supply, etc.) mechanisation, market organisations, etc. Comparison of material with 'intellectual' investment very often shows that the cost of training is low when compared with that of other measures to promote rural development, while its effects may be more beneficial. There are therefore many telling arguments which can be advanced in favour of carrying out projects for the improvement of rural education.

The annual cost of training will allow for the maintenance and depreciation of accommodation and equipment, running costs, including staff salaries and wages (always the most important item of total costs), expenditure on textbooks, paper, laboratory equipment, etc. and student maintenance, if this is also provided by the educational system. Professor Svennilson's formula is a convenient way of showing expenditure for a given type of training. If P_a is the agricultural population needing training, α_i the percentage of this population to be trained at, for example, vocational training centres, t_i the ratio of teachers to fully trained students, W_i the teachers' average annual earnings, k_i expenditure on material equipment expressed as a proportion of expenditure on staff and n_i the duration of the course in years, the cost (C) of training (i) can be expressed as follows:

$$C_i = P_a \times \alpha_i \times t_i \times W_i (1 + K_i) \times n_i$$

The advantage of this formula is that it gives a clear picture of the various components responsible for increased education costs, viz. changes in:

1. The population requiring training (P_a)
2. The actual proportion of the population receiving training (α_i)
3. Training structures, particularly teacher/student ratios (t_i)
4. Teachers' salaries (W_i)
5. The proportion of expenditure on equipment to expenditure on staff (K_i)
6. The duration of the course.

This formula could also well be used to investigate methods of limiting the cost of training without affecting its quality, a matter of some urgency in most LDCs.

Both population growth and, to a large extent, the proportion of trained staff required, which is determined by economic objectives, are input data as far as the educational system is concerned. On the other hand the structure of education, and in particular teacher/student ratios, depends on the educational system. The value of t_i for a given course of training will depend on wastage, grade repetition, pass rates in examinations, etc.

It should be possible to reduce the teacher/student ratio by selecting well-motivated students who are resolved to pursue their training to a successful conclusion. Motivation is likely to be much higher in adult education than in full-time education for young people, who are not always free to make their own choice and whose ultimate aim is sometimes in any case to leave agriculture.

NOTES

INTRODUCTION

1. Or 'developing countries'. These countries will henceforth be referred to mainly by the abbreviation LDC.
2. FAO, 'Summary and main conclusions', *Provisional Indicative World Plan for Agricultural Development – a synthesis and analysis of factors relevant to world, regional and national agricultural development,* 2 vols. (Rome, 1970), p.15.
3. Donella H. Meadows *et al., The Limits to Growth, a report for the Club of Rome* (Universe Books, New York, 1972).
4. Edgar Faure *et al., Learning to Be* (Unesco-Harrap, 1972), p.146.
5. Ibid., p.182.
6. Ibid., p.77.
7. Louis Malassis, Le Mas de l'Huile, Montferrier, 34000 Montpellier, France.

CHAPTER 1

1. Meadows *et al.,* op. cit.
2. Ibid., p.142.
3. Rene Dumont, *L'utopie ou la mort* (Seuil, Paris, 1973).
4. Meadows *et al.,* op. cit.
5. Faure *et al.,* op. cit., pp.235-63.
6. Ibid., pp.87-8.
7. Louis Malassis, *Agriculture and the Development Process; tentative guidelines for teaching,* Education and Rural Development, 3 (Unesco, Paris, 1975).
8. Faure *et al.,* op. cit., p.60.
9. Ibid., p.57.
10. Ibid., p.14.
11. Ibid., p.10.
12. Ibid., p.56.
13. Ibid., p.83.
14. Ivan Illich, *Deschooling Society* (Harper and Row, New York, 1971).
15. Faure *et al.,* pp.33-4.
16. Ibid., p.38.
17. Ibid., p.43.
18. Ibid.
19. Ibid., p.50.
20. Ibid., p.52.
21. Ibid., pp.70-1.
22. Ibid., p.71.
23. Ibid., p.42.
24. Ibid., pp.41-2.
25. Louis Malassis, *Intellectual Investment in Agriculture for Economic and Social Development* (OECD, Paris, 1962).
26. FAO, op. cit., pp.54-5.
27. Ibid., p.56.
28. Malassis, op. cit.

CHAPTER 2

1. Malassis, *Agriculture and the Development Process.*
2. Ibid., p.15.
3. Ibid.
4. Ibid., pp.197-8.
5. Montague Yudelman, 'The Green Revolution', *The OECD Observer,* No. 52 (Paris, June 1971), pp.15-18, 27-30.

6. Meadows *et al.,* op. cit., p.146.
7. Ibid., pp.147-8.
8. FAO, *Report of the Special Committee on Agrarian Reform,* 16th session, Rome, 8-25 November 1971 (mimeographed).
9. Malassis, op. cit., p.140.
10. Ibid., p.167.
11. FAO, *Indicative World Plan.*
12. Ibid., p.15.
13. Ibid., p.16.
14. Ibid., p.10.
15. Meadows *et al.,* p.145.
16. Ibid., p.150.
17. Ibid., p.154.
18. Ibid., p.49.
19. Ibid., p.34.
20. Ibid., p.51.
21. Ibid., p.148.
22. Ibid., pp.51-2.
23. Ibid., p.151.
24. Louis Malassis, *Systèmes de production agricole and développement socio-économique* (in preparation).
25. Ibid.
26. OECD, 'Aid for research in agricultural development, *The OECD Observer,* no. 32 (Paris, February 1968), pp.12-15.
27. An extended family system in which the head of the family concedes land to children, grandchildren, nephews, servants, etc., in return for their labour on his own land in the morning, the afternoon being free for work on their land.
28. Figures supplied by FAO.
29. Yves Goussault, 'Intervention educative et animation dans les problèmes de développement rural', *Options Méditerranéennes* (Paris, August 1971), p.72.
30. Malassis, *Agriculture and the Development Process,* pp.234-5.

CHAPTER 3

1. FAO, *Indicative World Plan,* p.54.
2. Frederick H. Harbison, 'Human resources planning in modernizing economies', *International Labour Review,* vol. LXXXV, no. 5 (Geneva, May 1962), p.444.
3. Faure *et al.,* op. cit., p.183.
4. Ibid., p.185.
5. Ibid., p.160 *et seq.*
6. Ibid., p.70.
7. Torsten Hussén, *Social Background and Educational Career; Research Perspectives on Equality of Educational Opportunity* (OECD, Paris, 1972).
8. Faure *et al.,* op. cit., pp.73-4.
9. Husén, op. cit., p.160.
10. Ibid., p.162.
11. Louis Malassis, 'Education and agricultural development', International Social Science Journal, vol. XXI, no. 2 (Paris, 1969), pp.244-55.
12. Faure *et al.,* op. cit., p.77.
13. Ibid., pp.105-44.
14. Ibid., pp.120-1.
15. Ibid., p.119.
16. Ibid., pp.78-9.
17. Ibid., pp.52-3.
18. Ibid., p.220.

19. Meadows *et al.,* op. cit.
20. FAO, op. cit.
21. Faure *et al.,* op. cit., p.209.
22. FAO, Unesco, ILO, World Conference on Agricultural Education and Training, Copenhagen, 28 July – 8 August 1970, *Report,* 2 vols. (FAO, Rome 1971)
23. V.L. Griffiths, *The Problems of Rural Education,* Fundamentals of Educational Planning, 7 (Unesco: International Institute for Educational Planning, Paris, 1969).
24. Mr Carel, who was kind enough to read over this text before publication, is preparing a study of this question.
25. Faure *et al.,* op. cit., p.164.
26. Louis Malassis, *Economic Development and the Programming of Rural Education* (Unesco, Paris, 1966).
27. Faure *et al.,* op. cit., p.175.
28. Institut international de planification de l'education, 7 rue Eugène Delacroix, 75016 Paris.
29. OECD Centre for Educational Research and Innovation, *Alternative Educational Futures in the United States and in Europe* (Paris, 1972).
30. Faure *et al.,* op. cit., p.xxxvii.
31. FAO, Unesco, ILO, *Report.*

APPENDIX

1. FAO, *Indicative World Plan,* vol. 2, p.427.
2. Ibid., p.428.

INDEX

Africa, 13, 40, 44, 57, 58, 83, 99
Agricultural colleges, 93
Agricultural development, 9-10, 19-20; and population growth, 17-19; new high yielding plants in, 53-4; necessity for intensification of, 58; extension services in, 69-71; measurement of success in, 71-2; need for, 75-6; stages in, 104-6
Agricultural education, still influenced by Western models, 48-9; how to integrate with general education, 96-7; how to improve training of personnel, 97-9; teaching methods in 109-11
Agricultural extension services, 49-50, 52-3, 92-3; role of, 67-9; various methods used by, 69-71; evaluating success of, 71-2
Agricultural extension workers, training of, 117-18
Agricultural land, area per person, 18, 58, 59
Agricultural population, as percentage of total populations, 13, 14-15; effects of continuing rise in, 57-8; estimating size of, 114-15
Agricultural production systems, 65-6; classification, 62-4; assessment of, 64-5
Agricultural societies, development in described, 36; land ownership in, 37; transformed by Western colonialism, 38; reasons for low productivity in, 52-3
Agricultural training, basic components of, 108-9
Agriculture, 112; development in the West, 14, 37; role in national development, 19; archaic forms of, 19-20; system of investment in formulated, 50; role in economic growth, 55-6; must attract more personnel, 107
Agriculture and the Development Process (quoted), 34-5
Animal production, 58
Animation, 70
Arab States, 44, 83
Asia, 13, 16, 40, 44, 57, 58
Australia, 17

Author, aims of, 25-6

Basic training, through primary schools, 89-91; new approaches to, 91-2
Bolivia, 68

Cereals, 34, 54, 58
Chile, 68
China, 91, 95
Club of Rome, 27
Computers, 111
Creation-dissemination process, 33-5, 46; co-ordination and control in, and present state of, 61-2; measuring results of, 72; farmer's role in, 72-3; is basis for economic growth, 85; in education, 102-4
Cuba, 95

Denmark, 68

Economic Development and the Programming of Rural Education, 7, 25
Economic growth, trends in LDCs, 16-17; limitations to, 27-8; *per capita,* 28-30; reasons for inequalities in, 30-2; factors in, 32; importance of technical progress in, 33; as process of destruction, 35; effect on agriculture, 51; role of creation-dissemination process in, 85; stages in, 104-6; needs integration of rural world, 107
Education, aims for, 11, 35; aims of Western system unsuited to LDCs, 20-1; reasons for low rural standards, 21; education on rural basis no answer, 21-2; aims in developing societies, 22-3; importance of adult education, 23-5; forms of decided by socio-economic systems, 38-9; aims of Western form and failure of, 39-40; can influence society, 41; efficiency discussed, 44; rising costs of, 45; disparities between social groups, 44; failing to meet needs of rural world, 48; must show importance of agriculture, 51; role in development process, 75;

aims in current world crisis, 77-8; causes of inequality in, 80-1; research in, 82-4; concepts must be widened, 84-5; 'package project' principle in, 94-5; integration of technical agricultural training in, 96; planning in, 99-100; future trends in, 101-2; needs to be integrated to be effective, 107-8; costs of, 120-2

Educational development, stages in, 104-6

Educational systems, should be adapted to each country, 31; term explained and structure defined, 42-3; current ones criticised, 43; concepts behind, 78-80; part of life-long education in, 80; inequality in, 80-1; removing inequality in, 81-2; planning for, 100-1; models for future systems, 101; assessment of by creation-dissemination process, 102-4

England, 37; land reform in, 19
Environment, 10
Estate managers, 18
Europe, 13, 44
Exports, 31

FAO, 13, 49, 113, 118; forecasts, 9
FAO Special Committee on Agrarian Land Reform, 55
Farmers, role in creation-dissemination process, 72-3
Faure, Edgar, 7
Feudal societies, 19, 37
First World Conference on Agricultural Education, 113
Fishing, 60
Food, 9-10
Food production, 18, 54, 56, 59, 60
Ford Foundation, 66
France, 66
French Revolution, 19, 37

Goussault, Yves, 70
Green Revolution, 20, 60, 66; new high yielding plants basis of, 54; benefits large-scale farmers, 54-5; where conditions are against, 55
Gross domestic product (GDP), 74
Gross national product (GNP), 60, 65; measured against education costs, 45
Guatemala, 68

Harbison, F.H. (quoted), 76

Heredity, laws of, 34
Husén, Professor Torsten, 81
Husén Report, 81

Illiteracy, 17, 43-4, 86, 109
ILO, 113
India, 54
Industrial Revolution, 37
Industrialisation, 16, 35, 37, 106
Intellectual investment system, 45-7
International Commission on the Development of Education, 7, 9, 23, 43, 112, 113
International Institute for Educational Planning, 100
International Maize and Wheat Improvement Centre, 54
International Programme for Educational Innovation, 12, 113
International relations, 31
Inventors, 33

Japan, 41, 65
Joint Advisory Committee on Agricultural Education, Science and Training, 113

Knowledge, outdated needs to be discarded, 46-7

Land, flight from to towns, 76-7
Landowners, 18
Land ownership, in agricultural societies, 37
Land tenure, 38
Latin America, 16, 38, 40, 44, 45
Learning to Be, 7, 9, 11, 12, 25
Less developed countries (LDCs), 52; populations increasing, 13-16; conditions in, 17-18; possibilities for economic growth, 27-9; and colonial powers, 31, 38; have adopted Western educational concepts, 40-1, 75; unbearable cost of education in, 45; education failing to meet needs of rural sector, 47; low standards of education in, 49; agricultural research in, 65; agricultural extension services in, 68-9; education of women in, 94; treat agricultural education as special category, 96-7
Life-long education, 12, 47, 80, 110-11; aims and role in national development, 23-5; structure explained, 42-3; best hope for

educational equality, 81-2; in rural environment, 93-4; should be corner-stone of educational system, 112

Malassis, Professor Louis, 7
Mali, 68
Malthus, 36
Market-orientated agriculture, 105, 106
Massachusetts Institute of Technology, 61
Meadows Report, 18, 27-8, 30, 60-1, 85; quoted, 58-60
Mexico, 54

Natural resources, 10, 59-60; limits to, 28
Near East, 57
Netherlands, 68
New Zealand, 17
North America, 44, 83

OECD Centre for Educational Research and Innovation (CERI), 81, 100-1

Pakistan, 54
Peasants, 16, 18
Personnel, training of, 96-9, 117-18, 119-20
Philippines, 54
Population growth, 9-10, 13, 17-19, 30, 59
Poverty belts, 10
Primary schools, 106; enrolment at, 43; importance of, 87-8; attendance at and unfair judgement of, 88-9; functions of, 89-91; reform of, 91
Production units, 46
Productivity, 30; necessity of increasing, 19; how to distribute benefits of, 31-2; how savings from should be invested, 46; of agricultural labour, 56
Protein deficiency, 58
Provisional Indicative World Plan for Agricultural Development (IWP), 13, 18, 57-8, 60-1, 85, 94, 110, 118; (quoted), 75-6

Research, and development, 34; expenditure on, 65; in LDCs, 65-6; better organisation of suggested, 66-7; implementation of results, 67-8; role of extension services in, 67-9

Rockefeller Foundation, 66
Rural development, 104-6
Rural education, 9; need for development of, 75-6; must be integrated with general education, 76-8; present isolation of, 86-7
Rural population, as percentage of total populations, 13-16; low share in economic growth benefits, 74; community development in, 95-6

Scales of growth, 27
Schools, changing role of, 42
Schumpeter, J., theories of, 35
Senegal, 68
Sinking fund, 46
Social security, new system needed, 47
Subsistence farming, 57-8, 64, 89, 105
Synthetic food, 60

Teaching methods, 109-11; need for improvement in, 82-4
Technical progress, process behind, 33-5; effects of acceleration of, 35
Technology, 62
Television sets, 83
Towns, attract rural population, 10
Tunisia, 54
Turkey, 54

Unesco, 7, 9, 51, 100, 113
United Nations Conference on Trade and Development (UNCTAD), 32
United States, 65
Urbanisation, 13
USSR, 13, 41

Vocational training, 92-3, 116-7
Venezuela, 68
Western societies, 48; aims of educational system, 20-1, 22, 39-40; development of, 16, 17, 33, 35-6, 37-8; teaching methods of, 82
Women, education of, 94

Zambia, 68